The Queer Mental
Health Workbook

of related interest

Trans Survival Workbook
Owl Fisher and Fox Fisher
ISBN 978 1 78775 629 8
eISBN 978 1 78775 630 4

The Trans Self-Care Workbook
A Colouring Book and Journal for Trans and Non-Binary People
Theo Lorenz
ISBN 978 1 78775 343 3
eISBN 978 1 78775 344 0

Hell Yeah Self-Care!
A Trauma-Informed Workbook
Alex Iantaffi and Meg-John Barker
ISBN 978 1 78775 245 0
eISBN 978 1 78775 246 7

The Anxiety Book for Trans People
How to Conquer Your Dysphoria, Worry Less and Find Joy
Freiya Benson
ISBN 978 1 78775 223 8
eISBN 978 1 78775 224 5

THE QUEER MENTAL HEALTH WORKBOOK

A Creative Self-Help Guide Using CBT, CFT and DBT

Dr Brendan J Dunlop

Jessica Kingsley Publishers
London and Philadelphia

First published in Great Britain in 2022 by Jessica Kingsley Publishers
An imprint of Hodder & Stoughton Ltd
An Hachette Company

1

Trigger warning: This book mentions abuse, anxiety, depression, eating disorders, self-harm, suicide, stress and trauma.

Disclaimer: The information contained in this book is not intended to replace the services of trained medical professionals or to be a substitute for medical advice. You are advised to consult a doctor on any matters relating to your health, and in particular on any matters that may require diagnosis or medical attention.

A CIP catalogue record for this title is available from the British Library and the Library of Congress

ISBN 978 1 83997 107 5
eISBN 978 1 83997 108 2

Printed and bound in the United Kingdom by TJ Books Ltd

Jessica Kingsley Publishers' policy is to use papers that are natural, renewable and recyclable products and made from wood grown in sustainable forests. The logging and manufacturing processes are expected to conform to the environmental regulations of the country of origin.

Jessica Kingsley Publishers
Carmelite House,
50 Victoria Embankment,
London, EC4Y 0DZ, UK

www.jkp.com

MIX
Paper from
responsible sources
FSC® C013056

Contents

PART 2: SPECIFIC MENTAL HEALTH DIFFICULTIES

Acknowledgements

This book hugely benefited from the thoughts, input, opinions and constructive criticism of the following fantastic individuals:

Dr Ben Campbell	Dr Peter Taylor
Rosy Wilson	Jennifer Fleming
Dr Alex Williams	Dr Roshini Prince-Navaratnam
Gail Quartly-Bishop	Dr Ian Gill
Dr Talen Wright	Dr Richard Falcon
Reiss Akhtar	Dr Katy Bourne
Dr Vanessa Fay	

Dr James Lea (BSc, DClinPsy, SFHEA) (he/they) co-authored the *Relationships* and *Intersectionality* chapters. James is a principal clinical psychologist, dialectical behaviour therapist (DBT), group work practitioner, clinical researcher and supervisor. At present, he works as Admissions Director and Clinical Tutor in clinical psychology at The University of Manchester and has a private practice offering psychotherapy and supervision to individuals and groups. He previously held the post of clinical lecturer at Bangor University and has worked clinically in a variety of NHS services. His research focuses on qualitative explorations within gender, sexuality and relationship diversity (GSRD) groups, self-harm and suicide. James has passion and expertise working psychologically with marginalized and oppressed groups, in particular those people who identify as belonging to the GSRD and/or LGBTQIA+ communities.

PART 1

BEING QUEER

— Chapter 1 —

INTRODUCTION

To be lesbian, gay, bisexual, transgender, queer, intersex, asexual, non-binary, pansexual (LGBTQ+) or anything other than heterosexual ('straight') and/or cisgender (identification with the sex you were assigned at birth) is to feel different. This does not just happen – people feel different and 'othered' because they notice that the world is not really designed for them. The assumption and dominant narrative that exists in the Global North is that all people are cishet (cisgender and heterosexual). A felt sense, even from a very young age, that you do not fit in can be incredibly difficult. The fallout from this can stick around for years. Many LGBTQ+ people grow up thinking that there is something inherently wrong with them, and this can become internalized. This can leave LGBTQ+ people with difficult-to-manage emotions arising from living in a discriminatory and unbalanced world.

This book aims to help LGBTQ+ people explore aspects of their identity, psychological wellbeing and mental health experiences at their own pace. I recognize that LGBTQ+ people reading this will all have different life experiences and different social systems around them and have developed different responses to these experiences, people, systems and stories. Because of this, there will be variation in where different people feel they identify on the spectrum of mental health and wellbeing.

Language is incredibly important in shaping our experiences. To this end, I have tried to choose the words I use carefully. For example, you will not see the term 'mental illness' or 'mental disorder' used in this book, because I think such phrases have some negative connotations. These descriptions were often used to refer to people who were admitted to 'asylums', and the perception was that such people could be unpredictable, or even dangerous. It was not until 1967 that homosexuality was removed as a 'mental illness' from the *Diagnostic and Statistical Manual* (the DSM; the manual psychiatrists use to diagnose people with mental health 'disorders'). Shockingly, it was only in 2013 when 'gender identity disorder' was replaced with gender dysphoria (the distress caused by a mismatch between someone's gender identity and their sex assigned at birth). Of course, even having 'transness' associated with the DSM is heavily contested, as why should being trans be framed as a 'difficulty' or 'disorder'?!

Instead, you will see me refer to 'mental health difficulties'. I think this is much more representative of what is actually going on – someone is having a difficult time with their mental health. It does not mean that they are ill or disordered, it just means things are rocky at the moment, and that things have happened to them which have been difficult to deal with. This is the basis for the Power Threat Meaning Framework (Johnstone & Boyle, 2018), one of the psychological approaches I have drawn on to influence this book. I recognize that some people do identify with the term 'mental illness' or 'mental disorder' and use this. If this is relevant and helpful for you to understand your experiences, then absolutely use this.

I should also justify why I have chosen to use the term 'Queer' throughout this book. While this term has historical negative connotations (it was used as a slur towards LGBTQ+ people for many years) the LGBTQ+ community has begun to reclaim this word as a symbol of identity and power – an example of the changeable nature of the stories and words that exist around us. Some within the LGBTQ+ community think of and identify with Queer as an independent group of people. I completely recognize and respect this. While not wishing to invalidate or erase the identity of those who identify with this term as distinct from other parts of the community, I have used the term Queer in this book to represent all those who are not cisgender and/or heterosexual.

I have included chapters on mental health difficulties that are either important to consider within the Queer community, or that Queer people are disproportionately affected by. This includes topics such as self-harm, eating difficulties, trauma and suicide. It goes without saying that these topics could be triggering for some people. If these difficulties are relevant for you and you would like to learn more about helping yourself with them, it may be a good idea to start with other chapters of the book first. This will allow you to develop your skills before you read these sections.

Ideas, theories and activities within this book have been selected from a variety of mental health and psychological approaches. Such theories and activities are primarily informed by Cognitive Behavioural Therapy (CBT), Compassion-Focused Therapy (CFT), Dialectical Behaviour Therapy (DBT) and, as mentioned earlier, the Power Threat Meaning Framework. There are also activities that draw on ideas from Narrative Therapy, Mindfulness, Systemic Therapy, Cognitive Analytic Therapy (CAT), and Acceptance and Commitment Therapy (ACT). A brief explanation of all these therapies and approaches is provided within the glossary in the next chapter. The reason I have taken such a broad approach and incorporated lots of different therapeutic ideas and approaches is because everyone is different! Focusing on just one approach may work for some, but not others. Therefore, it is my hope that by giving you a broad range of activities, based on different approaches, this will increase the likelihood that you will find something useful for you. Of course, the trade-off is that I will not be going into tons of detail about how each specific therapeutic approach would think about, understand and assist with each of the difficulties I will present. I hope you will be able to 'pick and mix' different activities from different therapies which are helpful for you, which you can then go away and read more about, if you wish.

HOW TO USE THIS BOOK

This book is designed for people who are not heterosexual and/or cisgender. The Queer community is a broad and heterogenous group, with different experiences, challenges and societal beliefs associated with each identity. Because this book highlights issues pertinent to being non-heterosexual and/or non-cisgender, most techniques and practices are intended to be applicable to any Queer person. This book is designed to be your own mental health and wellbeing resource, so feel free to scribble, draw and highlight bits that are relevant for you.

Not all parts of this book will be relevant for you. Because of this, I have designed the book so that each section can stand alone, meaning you can jump to the relevant bit for you, your identity and your needs. I would recommend at least reading Chapter 3, *Queer Mental Health: The Basics*, as this will give you an introduction to some of the ideas and exercises that will be presented in other chapters. On occasion, I will talk about an activity that may be useful, but refer to another chapter which covers it in some more detail.

Reading this book in its entirety may have additional benefits though. You may, for example, come across techniques or activities that are beneficial for you that you have not seen before. Do not feel obliged to complete all of the activities that are included within this book. Some people may find it equally as helpful to just read, learn and reflect.

There are activities throughout which allow you space to write down things that are applicable just for you. Activities are indicated with a grey bar containing the word 'activity' like this:

▶ ACTIVITY

Some activities have associated worksheets or diaries; there are additional blank copies available to download, which are marked with a ⊙ and can be accessed from https://library.jkp.com/redeem using the voucher code EKQRFKJ

Chapters end with a summary of what has been included, with five key 'takeaway' bullet points. Finally, there will be space for you to jot down any of your own reflections or thoughts. Or you can just scribble on these pages, or draw on them. Whatever you want!

At the end of the book there is a collection of resources, websites, helplines and email addresses for you to use if you wish. Helplines, websites and email addresses are all correct and valid at the time of publishing this book, though things of course change as time goes on so it is worth double checking these before using them.

WHAT THIS BOOK IS NOT

While the aim of this book is to help you understand your experiences and improve your psychological wellbeing and mental health, there are of course limitations that come with a self-help book. To that end, it is worth highlighting the following:

1. This book is not a definitive and conclusive set of issues and experiences that all Queer people may face. Just as there is so much variation within the Queer community, there will be things relevant to some that just are not relevant to others.

2. This book is not a total replacement for therapy or therapeutic intervention. Because you may be working through or consulting this book yourself, there is little opportunity to discuss how you are getting on

with others (although this is encouraged if you feel comfortable doing so!). Therapy offers something different from a self-help book.

3. This book may not be applicable or helpful to every Queer person. There may be techniques or activities that are not going to be useful or helpful for you, and that is OK. It is important to find a resource that works best for you. It is my aim to include a variety of different therapeutic approaches, techniques and activities so that there is a greater chance that something may be useful for you. Just because a particular difficulty I have included may commonly affect Queer people, this does not mean that you will or have experienced this. Everyone's journey and story is different!

4. This book is not an absolute discharge of responsibility for your own behaviour. As Queer people, we may not have asked for the cards that we were dealt, but what we do with those cards is our responsibility and choice. We may at times feel rage, anger and despair at the way the world and others have left us feeling, and there are healthy ways to manage this.

5. This book is not perfect. I have tried to be sensitive, inclusive and compassionate in the way that I have written and presented topics and activities. Sometimes, you may feel that I have not got something quite right. Or sometimes you may feel that I have missed something important. For this I apologize in advance, and hope you can understand my otherwise good intent.

6. Finally, this book *does not constitute clinical advice*. It is, of course, impossible for me to provide clinical advice to someone I have not met. Everyone is unique and different, and therefore I trust that you will select activities and exercises to try that you are comfortable with. If these do not work for you, I also trust that you will try something else. If something seems to be making things worse, I also trust that you will disengage from this and try something different.

Because I have written this from my own perspective, it was important for me to try and ensure that what I was writing about was relevant to a range of people from the Queer community. For this reason, people from a broad range of identities, with a broad range of experiences, have also had input into this book. This may have been checking the wording I have used, suggesting activities that they found useful for their own mental health or ensuring that activities are relevant for a broad range of Queer people. A list of all people who provided input into this book can be found in the Acknowledgements section. I am forever grateful to them for their honesty and input.

It can sometimes be quite a lot to learn about and unpack bits of your identity and experience that you might not have thought much about. Take this book easy, go at your own pace and be kind to yourself. It can take time to improve our mental health. If things are not going well at the moment, or you try some things and they do not work right away, just remember that *waves will still crash on the shore tomorrow*. There is always a chance to try something else.

Wishing you all the best.
Brendan

Chapter 2

GLOSSARY

Below is a glossary of some of the terms used throughout the book. This starts off by explaining what some of the psychological therapies and approaches are that I have drawn on for the content of this book. Towards the end there are some Queer-specific words that you might not have heard before (or might have, but are not sure what they mean).

PSYCHOLOGICAL THERAPIES AND PSYCHOLOGICAL APPROACHES

Acceptance and Commitment Therapy (ACT) (Hayes, Strosahl & Wilson, 2012) This was developed by Steven Hayes and uses mindfulness and self-acceptance techniques to encourage the development of psychological flexibility. By moving towards difficulties and stresses, rather than avoiding them, people 'commit' to tackling these head on.

Cognitive Analytic Therapy (CAT) (Ryle, 1995) This focuses on the importance of relationships and the roles we have within them. These relationships can be with ourselves, with others and with wider society/culture/groups. Sometimes we find ourselves in unhelpful relational patterns, and by becoming aware of these patterns, we can begin to do something about them.

Cognitive Behavioural Therapy (CBT) (Beck, 1964) CBT is based on the idea that thoughts, feelings and behaviours are connected. Therefore, if we change the way that we think, this can have an impact on how we feel, and what we do. Equally, changing our behaviour can lead to changes in feelings and thoughts.

Compassion-Focused Therapy (CFT) (Gilbert, 2010) CFT is largely attributed to Paul Gilbert. Central to CFT is the idea that psychological and emotional healing can come about through compassion towards the self, and towards other people.

Dialectical Behaviour Therapy (DBT) (Linehan, 1993) Created by Marsha M. Linehan in the USA, DBT was developed primarily to help people who struggled with suicidal and self-harming behaviours, as a result of emotional dysregulation.

DBT is a skills-based therapy, helping people develop skills in tolerating distressing feelings and communicating effectively in their relationships. A central idea in DBT is that of 'dialectics' – the idea that there can be two 'opposing' truths that are equally valid, and can co-exist (e.g., 'I want to tell someone what has happened to me' and 'I never want to tell anyone what happened.' These are opposing truths, and both can be equally valid).

Fight or flight response This is our body's natural and automatic threat detection system. Because our brains have evolved over millions of years, this part of our 'animal' brain can become activated even when there is no 'real' threat. Fight or flight is more fully explained in Chapter 8, *Feeling Anxious*.

Mindfulness (Kabat-Zinn, 1982, 1990) Originating in Eastern Buddhist philosophy, and 'brought to the West' by Jon Kabat-Zinn, mindfulness is a meditation practice. Mindfulness involves paying attention to experiences, in a non-judgemental and purposeful way.

Narrative Therapy (White & Epston, 1990) Developed primarily by Michael White and David Epston, this places emphasis on 'dominant' stories that exist in society: those stories that we tell ourselves and that others tell us. When these stories become rooted, they can leave little room for consideration of other stories or narratives that can or could exist. For example, if someone once crashed their car, they may become known as the 'car crasher', and this story may become the focus of conversation whenever this person is around. Opportunities to develop a narrative that is anything other than the 'car crasher' are limited. Because of this, mental health difficulties (linked to feelings such as shame, feeling anxious etc.) can result from this dominant story. Narrative Therapy aims to help develop alternative, more helpful stories.

Power Threat Meaning Framework (Johnstone & Boyle, 2018) A psychological framework developed by Lucy Johnstone and Mary Boyle as an alternative to the current psychiatric diagnostic system. This framework suggests that power exists within societies (e.g., heteronormativity, patriarchy, white supremacy) which creates a threat (e.g., 'I am different, how do I fit in?') that we respond to in some way (e.g., learn different ways of fitting in that others do not do). This is linked to the meaning we attribute to this power, including the way we have responded.

Systemic Therapy (de Shazer, 1985; Selvini-Palazzoli *et al.*, 1978, 1980) Typically a form of family therapy, Systemic Therapy aims to alleviate psychological distress and conflict by bringing awareness to the relationships, spoken and unspoken rules and routines, and interactions between people and the systems around them. While such a system could be a family unit, it could also be larger systems such as workplaces, institutions or communities.

QUEER-SPECIFIC, OR QUEER-RELEVANT TERMINOLOGY

Cisgender A person whose gender identity fits with the sex they were assigned at birth.

Cishet Someone who is both cisgender and heterosexual; a blend of these two words.

Gender dysphoria The psychological distress that someone experiences because the sex they were assigned at birth does not fit with their sense of gender identity.

Gender euphoria The elation that someone feels about their gender identity.

Heteronormative The idea that the assumption of heterosexuality is the default position. Therefore social stories, institutions, policies and laws are centred around this assumption of 'heteronormativity'.

Queer Originally, 'queer' was simply used to describe something that was different. For example, if someone was wearing a funny looking hat, you might say, 'What a queer hat that person is wearing!' Over time, the word 'queer' came to be negatively associated with someone who was not heterosexual. This became an abusive and derogatory term. For this reason, there are still some people who do not like using this word. More recently, some sections of the LGBTQ+ community have come to reclaim (take back control over) this word, and it is now often used to describe someone who is not cisgender and/or heterosexual. Some people within the LGBTQ+ community specifically identify as 'queer' and use this to describe their sexual orientation and/or gender identity.

Transgender A person whose gender identity did not, or does not, fit with their sex assigned at birth.

Chapter 3

QUEER MENTAL HEALTH: THE BASICS

The basic principles that I want to highlight in this chapter are by no means the *only* principles of mental health and wellbeing. Rather, these are principles I have selected based on my professional identity and position as a Clinical Psychologist and my personal point of view of what may be most helpful for Queer people. I think it is probably most helpful to start with thinking about ourselves as individuals, and then we can move on to consider ourselves within a broader context afterwards. To only consider individual difficulties divorced of a wider context is, in my opinion, to not fully understand the development and maintenance of a difficulty. That being said, I absolutely understand that sometimes we cannot always change the context or external factors that are around us, but we can change how we approach or manage our responses to these.

THOUGHTS, FEELINGS AND BEHAVIOURS ARE CONNECTED: THE HOT CROSS BUN

Have you ever noticed how sometimes you think about something that is worrying you, such as an exam coming up, and suddenly you start to feel butterflies in your stomach? Or that when you are feeling sad and stay in because you think your friends do not want to see you, you end up feeling worse? That is because we now know that our thoughts, feelings and behaviours are intimately connected and influence (and are influenced by) each other. This theory forms the basis of a psychological therapy approach that you may have heard of: Cognitive Behavioural Therapy, or CBT (Beck, 1964). The specific understanding of the connections between thoughts, feelings and behaviours was further developed by Padesky and Mooney in 1990, and can be drawn out and understood as a 'hot cross bun' model (Padesky & Mooney, 1990). This model shows how thoughts, feelings, behaviours and physical sensations are linked to each other, and how one element is often connected to each of the other three. Here is an example of a young transwoman I shall call 'Leah':

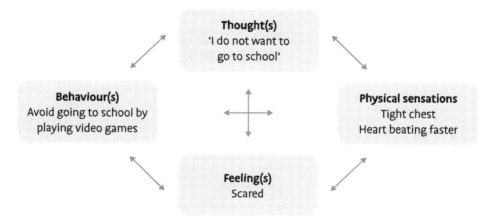

Figure 3.1: Example 'hot cross bun' of Leah, who does not want to go to school

When Leah gets the thought that she does not want to go to school, she notices that her chest feels tight and her heart is beating faster. That thought, along with these physical sensations, can lead to intense feelings of being scared. Because of these three things, Leah does something to try make things better for herself, just as we all would. She stays inside and plays video games. Phew! That stopped her feeling scared, and now her chest feels better and her heart rate has gone down. Maybe she now thinks, 'I am safe here at home!' While this behaviour helped Leah manage her thoughts, feelings and physical sensations *at that point in time*, it can quickly become problematic. For example, next time Leah has to go to school she may experience the same thoughts, feelings and sensations. Last time this happened, staying at home and playing video games made her feel much better. This behaviour has *reinforced* ('made stronger') the idea that school is scary, because she never ended up going to school and being (hopefully) proved wrong. Over time, we can learn to recognize how the interaction between thoughts, feelings, physical sensations and behaviours can keep us 'stuck' in patterns of behaving in ways that may help us feel better for a very short while, but ultimately have unhelpful consequences (Leah cannot stay away from school forever as she needs to learn for her exams, but school is feeling scarier and scarier each day).

Noticing how your thoughts, feelings, physical sensations and behaviours interact with each other can be incredibly helpful in breaking unhelpful cycles. Below is a blank diagram – why not have a go at filling this in with a recent difficult or unpleasant event? If it is tricky to remember what was going through your head, start with what you felt in your body, or what emotions stick out for you. Behaviours can also be things you actively did (such as removed yourself from a situation, or ended a phone call) but can also be things you did not do (such as avoiding an activity or person, or not going out). It is OK if you cannot think of anything now, or if you only have one or two boxes filled in. You can return to this activity later if you like, once you have read a bit more.

ACTIVITY

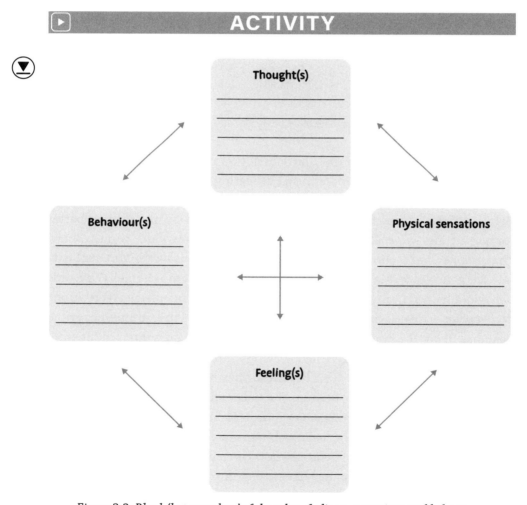

Figure 3.2: Blank 'hot cross bun' of thoughts, feelings, sensations and behaviours

SITUATING PERSONAL WELLBEING WITHIN A BROADER CONTEXT: THE CIRCLES OF INFLUENCE

In Leah's 'hot cross bun' example above, there could be many reasons why she did not want to go to school. Perhaps she was struggling to concentrate and had started to fall behind with her work. She did not want to be seen as 'stupid' by her friends, so she stayed at home instead. Or maybe she was being bullied, or thought that she might be bullied, because of her gender identity and the way she dressed, spoke or walked. When we zoom out and think about some of the reasons for Leah not wanting to go to school, we can start to understand or 'formulate' what might be underpinning this. While Leah could change some of her behaviours or some of her thoughts to make herself feel better, this may not be the only solution available.

Everybody has 'mental health'. Mental health can be thought of as encompassing our thoughts, feelings, aims and intentions, including how we respond to stress. Mental health and wellbeing is very much a spectrum, and we all fall somewhere on this spectrum with regard to our 'wellness'. This is not static either – we can experience mental health difficulties and improve our mental health, or go from stable mental health to poorer mental health.

| Fantastic mental health | OK/good mental health | Very poor mental health |

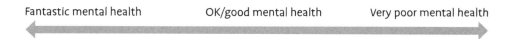

Because none (or at least very few!) of us live on remote abandoned islands by ourselves, our psychological wellbeing can very much be influenced by the world around us.

Throughout this book, I shall often make reference to the world around us when considering psychological wellbeing and mental health difficulties. In my opinion, there are three things in particular that are relevant for Queer people. These are the **people and groups** around us, the **institutions, laws and policies** of the country or society we live in, and **social stories**. To that end, it is worth me clarifying what I mean by these. When I say people and groups around us, I mean family systems, relationships between people, groups or organizations that we are a part of. **Institutions** often refer to physical places (such as a government or university building) or the social and cultural practices associated with physical buildings (organized religion being an example of an institution). **Laws and policies** refer broadly to the rules and accepted practices (created by powerful people) that are embedded within a society. And **social stories** refer to the things that are told to us, or that we assume to be true, because lots of people talk and think about them. Social stories can be passed down through generations, created or influenced by the media, told to us by others or created by ourselves.

For Queer people, there are many factors associated with these three broad categories that can influence our mental health. The extent to which these external influences are supportive, inclusive and tolerant can lead to very different outcomes. Let us think again about Leah, and consider some of these external factors if we zoom out a bit:

- **People and groups**, such as Leah's so-called 'friends', may have invalidated her identity because she was not cisgender.

- **Institutions, laws and policies** in Leah's home country discriminate against her very existence, with legal implications (e.g., not being legally recognized as a woman).

- **Social stories**, such as trans people being labelled as 'weird' or 'scary', might have led Leah to be shamed in sports classes by her teacher, who says that she 'plays football alright for a sissy in a dress'.

Alternatively, let us imagine Leah with a different set of external circumstances:

- **People and groups**, such as Leah's friends, have been welcoming and supportive of her Queer identity.

- **Institutions, laws and policies** in Leah's home country are respectful and welcoming of difference, and have anti-discrimination laws that prevent Queer people being discriminated against on the basis of their gender identity.

- **Social stories**, such as trans people being worthy of the same kindness, respect and compassion as everyone else, have led Leah's teacher to be actively zero-tolerant towards transphobia (harassment or discrimination because of her trans identity) in sports.

Thinking about these two examples, and without knowing anything about Leah, which do you think could lead to the more distressing mental health difficulties or threats to psychological wellbeing? I am assuming you may have thought that the first example would lead to more psychological distress.

I hope you can see that these external factors can have a real impact on someone's sense of safety, self-worth, confidence and thoughts about others. Thinking about these wider factors, there seem to be several reasons why Leah may, very understandably, not want to go to school! There are some things that Leah can do to make herself feel better, which I will explore in Chapter 8, *Feeling Anxious*. But it seems to me that there are other things that definitely need to change around Leah to make her life easier, because it is totally unfair that she is being treated that way. Throughout this book, I will try and highlight things that you as an individual can do to help yourself, but also ways in which you can try and change, or at least have influence over, some of the external conditions around you.

So why might Leah be having such a tough time at school? For Queer people, external influences may be repeatedly negative because the way in which modern society is built and structured favours people who fall into the 'status quo' – the status quo usually being white, able-bodied, heterosexual and cisgender ('cishet'; particularly cisgender men). So, *people and groups* can act in ways that are abusive and exclusionary to those whom they perceive 'not to be as worthy' as them, or 'too different'. *Institutions, laws and policies* may not wish to promote or celebrate identities that challenge white, able-bodied, heterosexual and cisgender privilege. *Social stories* are created to further ostracize Queer people and keep them oppressed and viewed negatively by society, such as the socially constructed (and politically motivated) narrative that transwomen are a threat to 'real women' and are simply 'violent predatory men out to abuse normal women in bathrooms and public spaces'. (Of course, they are absolutely NOT, and transwomen are much more likely to be the victim of a sexual and/or physical assault.) When you are Queer and are so obviously not part of the status quo, is it any wonder that there can be challenges and threats to your mental health? Leah is viewed as different, and people do not always like difference.

The following 'circles of influence' (based on ideas by Bronfenbrenner, 1977) demonstrate just some of the people and groups, institutions, laws and policies, and social stories that exist around us, and that can influence our wellbeing.

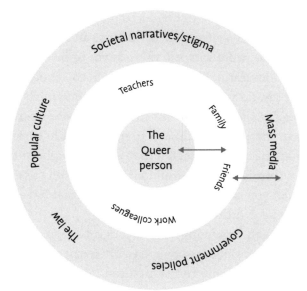

Figure 3.3: Circles of influence: external factors that exist around us, with bigger circles influencing smaller circles

Here is a broad example of how some of these circles of influence can 'trickle down' to impact on an individual Queer person:

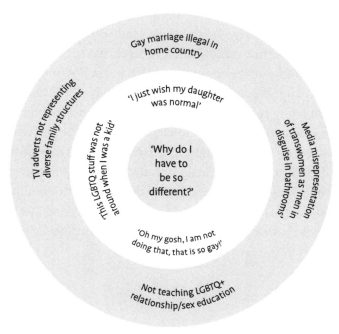

Figure 3.4: Circles of influence: how the world around us can influence wellbeing for Queer people

If you want to, and think it may be useful, use the following blank set of circles to jot down people or groups, institutions, laws and policies, or social stories that have influenced your wellbeing. It may also be helpful to draw arrows linking how various ideas within these circles have affected those around you, and ultimately yourself.

ACTIVITY

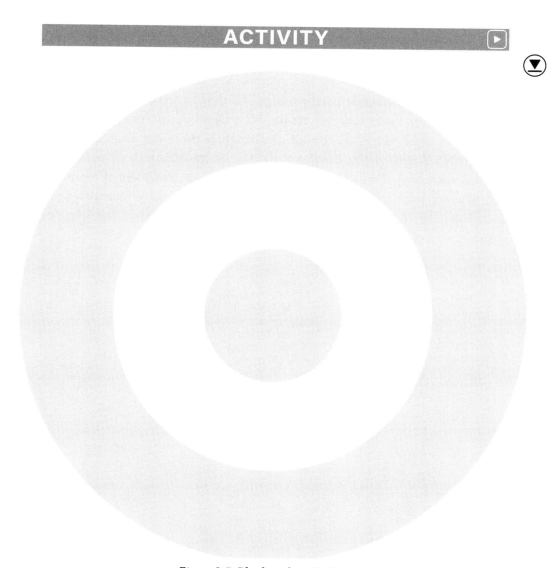

Figure 3.5: Blank circles of influence

MINORITY STRESS THEORY

Because there are so many circles of influence around us, there are multiple ways that these systems can affect our personal wellbeing and mental health. In Meyer's original (2003) *Minority Stress Theory,* it was theorized that being a sexual minority individual was an inherently stressful experience, due to stigma and discrimination resulting from interpersonal relationships and wider systems of influence (such as those described above). Meyer's original ideas were mainly based on sexual orientation; however, the same principle applies to gender identity.

This 'minority stress' can lead to shame and a variety of mental health difficulties. What can end up happening is that the mental health difficulties that follow from such minority stress can exhaust us and tire us out, leaving us with little energy to disrupt or dismantle these oppressive systems and stories. Additionally, having a mental health difficulty as a result of minority stress can be used as 'evidence' that Queer people are different, in turn keeping such difficulties going and feeding into the heteronormative and cisgender systems that initially fuelled this. I hope that the 'cycle of oppression' below will help put this into context:

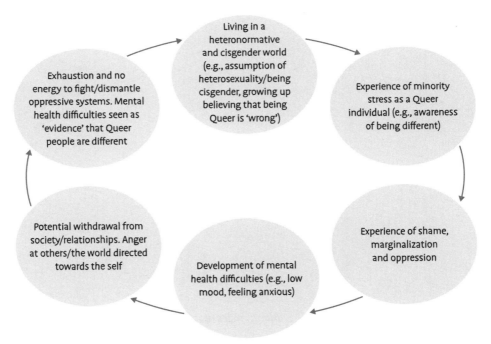

Figure 3.6: Cycle of oppression

It is important to highlight the cycle of oppression as this can help us visualize mental health difficulties and threats to wellbeing in context. It is worth noting that the above cycle is not unique to Queer people; a similar cycle exists for other marginalized and minoritized groups. Some people can develop a personal story that being different is wrong, and the resulting difficulties they are having are their fault. This can be reinforced by other people in their lives who remind them of this, or reiterate such ideas. Actually, when you zoom out a bit and look at such difficulties from a different angle, you can trace this back to influences much bigger than ourselves. It is not always easy to do this. People and groups invested in the status quo can feel threatened when we say that these systems and structures have limitations and need to change to become more inclusive. Systems and structures acknowledging their limitations and acknowledging that things need to be different can be a very threatening thing for some people to understand.

THOUGHTS, FEELINGS AND BEHAVIOURS IN CONTEXT

So, thoughts, feelings and behaviours are connected. We saw that for Leah. But as mentioned before, we do not live as isolated beings in this world. For Leah, let us assume the first example of external factors reflected what was going on for her. While Padesky & Mooney (1990) recognized the influence that the immediate environment had on our hot cross bun, we have explored some of the many things in the world around us that can have influence over our thoughts, feelings and behaviours. So, the circles of influence around us could be impacting on these, and we may (or may not) be aware of this. On the following page is a blank copy of a hot cross bun inside some circles. If you want to, write down an aspect of your experience that may be worrying or distressing you, and then write down any people or groups, institutions, laws and policies, or social stories that may be influencing or interacting with your difficult experience. You can use the same one you did earlier if you like, or think of something different. Drawing arrows between the various external influences and each area of your hot cross bun can be useful, so you can see which external influences are most influential.

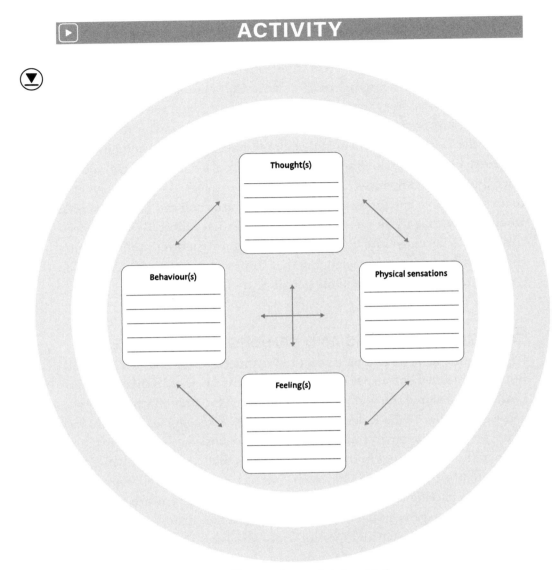

Figure 3.7: Hot cross bun and circles of influence

IMPROVING MENTAL HEALTH AND WELLBEING

As I mentioned before, there are a few different principles for improving our mental health and wellbeing. Broadly, these either focus on changing aspects of ourselves (such as how we are thinking, or what we are doing) or changing things around us.

To change things for ourselves, we can check if the way in which we are thinking is helpful for us. Is it keeping you up at night? Are these thoughts feeling really powerful and threatening? Is this thought trying to make you believe something that may not be true?

You could actively aim to challenge the thought, or perhaps you could try and leave the thought alone, almost as if you were watching it walk past you at the park. In the following diagram, I have included some ways that you could try managing your tricky thoughts, including trying to leave them alone.

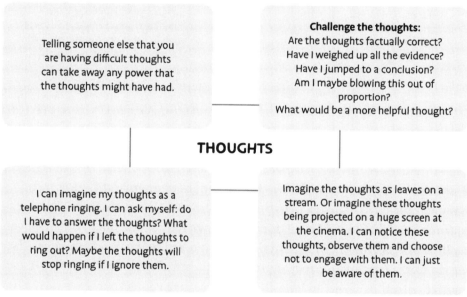

Figure 3.8: Ways of challenging and changing your tricky or unhelpful thoughts

When it comes to some of things we do ('behaviours'), there are things we can have a go at changing. Sometimes this might involve distracting ourselves when we can feel that we are about to do something unhelpful. Alternatively, we can tell other people about the things that we do that are ultimately not helpful for us, so that they can be our 'eyes and ears' and help us to recognize this and do something different. Just as I did with thoughts, I have included some ideas below that you could do to change behaviour.

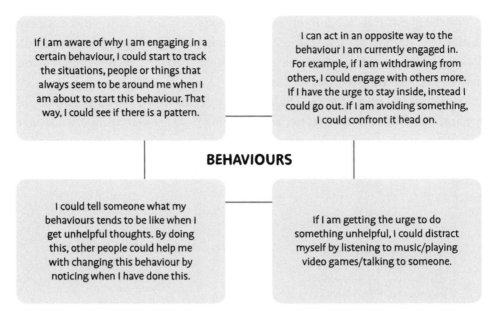

Figure 3.9: Ways of challenging and changing your tricky or unhelpful behaviour

When it comes to improving mental health and wellbeing by thinking about the influences around us, we need to be realistic about what we can achieve. Sometimes, trying to push for change where change just is not going to happen quickly can have a negative impact on us. There are, however, some options available to us. Some of these things may seem small, but they can really make a difference to mental health and wellbeing. For influences that we do not have much direct input into, such as laws and policies, we can engage with those who do hold the power. In situations that leave us feeling powerless, engaging with those who can make a difference can help us regain a sense of control.

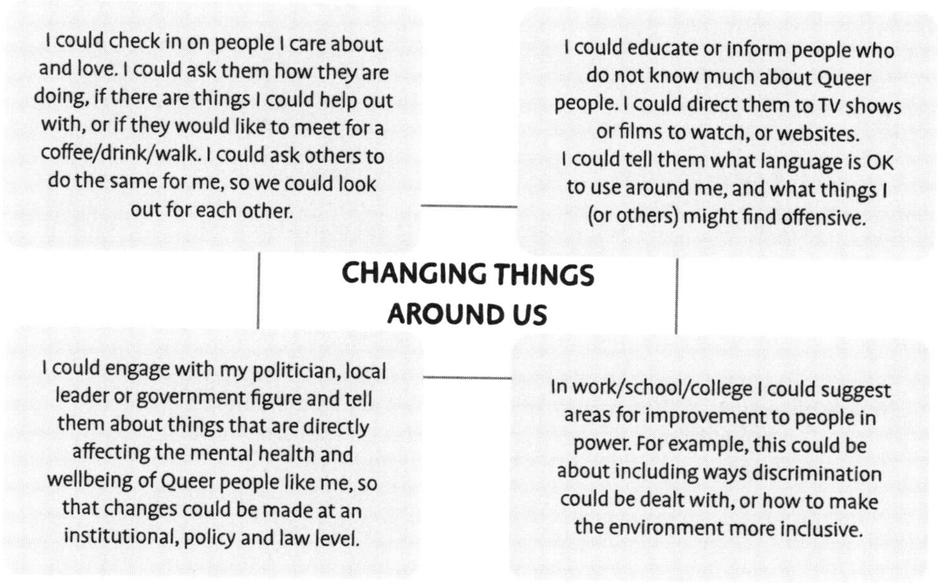

I could check in on people I care about and love. I could ask them how they are doing, if there are things I could help out with, or if they would like to meet for a coffee/drink/walk. I could ask others to do the same for me, so we could look out for each other.

I could educate or inform people who do not know much about Queer people. I could direct them to TV shows or films to watch, or websites. I could tell them what language is OK to use around me, and what things I (or others) might find offensive.

CHANGING THINGS AROUND US

I could engage with my politician, local leader or government figure and tell them about things that are directly affecting the mental health and wellbeing of Queer people like me, so that changes could be made at an institutional, policy and law level.

In work/school/college I could suggest areas for improvement to people in power. For example, this could be about including ways discrimination could be dealt with, or how to make the environment more inclusive.

Figure 3.10: Ways of challenging and changing the world around us

SETTING GOALS AND AIMS

A great way to be able to track progress, and feel motivated to improve our situations, can be to set a goal or an aim. Doing this is not for everyone. If you know you are someone who does not like setting goals, then skip this bit. For this particular book, setting a goal can help you decide what you want to work on, or change. Because of the way this book is structured, if there is a specific difficulty you want to work on, you can jump straight to that section. I have designed the table on the following page so that you can track your goal or aim by thinking about what is helping you work towards it, what is making it trickier and what you could try next. You can also rate (out of 10) where you feel you are at with your goal or aim. That way, you can come back to this table over time and track progress. Being specific about your goal, and where you want to get to, can help. I have included an example below, with a blank table afterwards for you to use yourself.

Table 3.1: Example goal tracker

Goal or aim: Improve my sleep

How will I know I have reached this goal or aim?: I will be able to sleep completely through without waking up

Rating: 1 = not made progress, 5 = halfway there, 10 = done it!

Date	What is helping	What is making it tricky	What I could try next	Rating out of 10
21 January	Having a routine	Smoking before bed	Try to reduce number of cigs I smoke from 5 to 2	3
1 February	Having a routine, cutting down on cigs	Started having nightmares	Continue cutting down cigs, try to calm myself down if I wake up from a nightmare by doing breathing exercises, rather than smoking	4
6 February	Practising mindfulness	I do not always fully understand how mindfulness should be helping me	Read up a bit more about mindfulness to see if that helps	4
16 February	Consistent mindfulness practice	I still get nightmares, which can make me feel like I am not making much progress	Be kind to myself by recognizing that my sleep is much better than it used to be, and also find out about talking to someone about my nightmares	7

ACTIVITY

Blank goal tracker

Goal or aim:

How will I know I have reached this goal or aim?:

Rating: 1 = not made progress, 5 = halfway there, 10 = done it!

Date	What is helping	What is making it tricky	What I could try next	Rating out of 10

I will revisit some of the basic principles introduced in this chapter through-out the book. I am hoping that you can hold them in mind as you read through. You can come back to this chapter at any time if you want to use any of these activities, exercises or information in other chapters.

— Chapter 4 —

IDENTITY

WHY CLAIMING AND EMBRACING A QUEER IDENTITY CAN BE DIFFICULT

Queer people grow up living in a world that constantly and systematically invalidates our identities. For example, have you ever heard or experienced any of the following?

- Gay people can be told that what we are going through is *just a phase*'.

- Lesbian women can be told that you *just have not found the right man yet*'.

- Bisexual people are often told to *pick a side*' or that you will *realize you are gay soon*'.

- Trans people, in particular trans kids, are often told that *you are confused*' or *have been hanging around with boys/girls too much*'.

- Non-binary or pansexual people are told you are *trying too hard to be different*'.

- Aromantic or asexual people are often told *you will change your mind when you meet the right person*'.

- Or *you are just making up more letters in the LGBT acronym*'.

Stereotypes such as 'gay people cannot drive or play sports' and social narratives of the camp gay best friend can lead us to question if there is anything more to us than this. Consequently, as Queer people we grow up not really knowing who we truly are, having either been forced to live a life we are not happy with, thinking that the very core of who we are is 'wrong' or that we are nothing more than the stereotype that society has created for us.

Of absolute importance is this: *you define who you are, not somebody else.*

It is OK if the way you define yourself changes over time. And it is also OK if you do not 'fit in' to a certain category. Society likes to place people into neat and tidy boxes for many reasons. One of these reasons, I think, is because it makes life feel more predictable: Queer identities outside the 'mainstream' threaten this predictability, by going against the grain of the dominant and pervasive assumptions of heteronormativity.

When people feel that something is not predictable, they are motivated to correct this, because unpredictability can threaten the 'status quo'. When the status quo is threatened, white, heterosexual, able-bodied, cisgender men worry that they will not be able to keep their historical grip on society and its structures (though this is not the only group that can be experienced as the 'status quo'; the trans community can experience this from cisgender men and women too). Thus, your identity is questioned, you are asked to select a box, and not change. When a Queer person feels a sense of uneasiness about their identity, maybe this uneasiness is representative of something much bigger. Perhaps this uneasiness 'belongs' instead to society and the rules and pressures it forces on Queer people? It can be a different way of thinking if you have not considered the power that the circles of influence have on your life before, and I encourage you to think about this if you feel it is relevant for you.

Thinking back to the 'circles of influence' introduced in the previous chapter, there are many things that can make us as Queer people feel ostracized, marginalized and alone. Because of this, many Queer people spend their adolescent and young adult lives working out who they really are. Which parts

DID YOU KNOW?

Up until 1967, homosexuality was illegal in the UK. Under the Sexual Offences Act (1967), homosexual acts were legalized.

Homosexuality is still criminalized in 72 countries worldwide.

Impact on mental health

Older people living in the UK today may remember a time when being gay (in particular) was *against the law*. This had (and has) powerful implications for the moral and ethical acceptability of being Queer. People's belief systems are likely to have been influenced by the law, then and now. Older Queer people in the UK may have internalized this sense of immorality and shame and never disclosed their true sexuality.

For people living in countries where being gay or Queer is criminalized, the explicit message is that your very existence is wrong and cannot be tolerated by society. Disclosing your true identity may compromise your safety. Internalizing this sense of stress, hypervigilance and immorality could lead to issues controlling your thoughts and emotions. Some people may even try take their own life if they see no other way out.

Your fault? Not at all.

of ourselves have potentially been created to please our families, friends, culture or faith? Which parts of ourselves have we always wanted to embrace, but could not? Which parts of ourselves have we grown to hate and despise, because we believe those parts are sinful, morally wrong or shameful? This can be one of the most painful and liberating experiences for Queer people.

Discovering who you truly are can mean confronting painful experiences, situating these in context, understanding why certain experiences may have happened and reclaiming the 'power' these social stories may hold over you. Identifying the defences you have built, or the parts of yourself you are trying to punish, can also help you understand why you may be feeling certain emotions, discomfort or distress. Once you begin to recognize this, and understand why you may be doing some of the things you do, you can start embracing the wonderfully Queer parts of yourself in a compassionate, non-judgemental and positive way. When you are reading some of the chapters in this book and completing some of the activities, I would encourage you to think about the relationship that particular difficulty may have with your identity as a Queer person. Importantly: who or what is making this particularly difficult *because of* your identity as a Queer person?

THINKING ABOUT MY IDENTITY IN CONTEXT

The questions below encourage you to think about your Queer identity in relation to the people and groups around you, the institutions, laws and policies that structure your life, and the social stories that exist in the society you live in. This can be a useful self-reflective exercise to begin to think about how the world around you interacts with your identity. As you move through this book, I encourage you to think about these questions in relation to specific difficulties you may have, to see if you can find any connections.

 ACTIVITY

People and groups

Do I know many Queer people? If so, what do I like about them and what do I dislike about them? Is that the type of person I want to be?

If I do not know many Queer people, would I like to?

Is there someone famous who is also Queer that I admire? Why?

Is being Queer accepted or celebrated by the people or groups I hang around with?

Is there anybody that I know who really brings out and celebrates the Queer parts of my identity?

Is there anybody I really want to invite into my Queer world, but worry that they will reject me? Why do I think they will reject me?

Thoughts, answers, reflections on these questions:

Institutions, laws and policies

If I am religious, does my religion or faith accept being Queer? If not, are there other denominations within my religion or faith that do accept being Queer?

If I am part of a sports club, do my teammates accept my being Queer? If not, what parts of me do I cover up that I do not want them to see? At what cost do I do this?

Are there any clubs, groups or organizations that I want to join, but have not yet done so? Is this connected to my being Queer?

Are there any clubs, groups or organizations that I am part of that celebrate being Queer? Am I able to fully embrace my Queer identity when in these spaces?

Are there laws or policies that exist to keep my Queer identity hidden? What do I do to cover up or hide the parts of myself that could jeopardize my safety? At what cost do I do this?

Thoughts, answers, reflections on these questions:

Social stories

What social stories exist about Queer people in my community? Are they positive or negative?

Have these social stories had any impact on the way I have embraced, or rejected, my Queer identity? Why?

If I could create a social story from scratch about being Queer, what would it be and why?

If we lived in a world free from discrimination, what parts of my Queer identity would I celebrate? Are there any of these parts that I feel able to connect with in the society I currently live in?

Thoughts, answers, reflections on these questions:

THE PRIVATE AND PUBLIC SELF

Our behaviour is often shaped by the environment that we are in. Because of this, there may be parts of our identity that we are happy to let others see, and parts of our identity that we are not. This is, by the way, totally normal! We do not have to show every part of us to other people.

Sometimes though, the environment or context we are in stops us from embracing the parts of ourselves that we wish we could show more often. One prime example that may be relevant to you as you read this book is actually embracing your Queerness or Queer identity – a core part of your identity you might really want to tell others about but do not feel able to yet (or cannot for whatever reason). By the way, in this book I do not refer to people as *coming out* as Queer. Instead, I refer to this process as *embracing your Queer identity*. This is because I think the term 'coming out' can have connotations of someone previously having been 'hiding' or 'not their true self'. 'Coming out' implies the need to publicly announce that we are the 'other' and must 'come out' to show we are not occupying space as others who conform to the 'norm' are. This is problematic and can make a Queer person feel unnecessarily bad (after all, if the world were so accepting of Queer people surely you would not even have to have this conversation). When others say that they 'had their suspicions' about your sexuality or gender identity, it makes me think, why is your identity something somebody was 'suspicious' of in the first place?! You are inviting other people to see this part of yourself, rather than 'coming out' into the heteronormative and cisgender world.

Alok Vaid-Menon, a gender non-conforming performance artist and poet, once asked: 'What feminine part of yourself did you have to destroy in order to survive in this world?' I think this is a powerfully important question for us all to reflect on. Another example of a part of your identity that you may wish to be public (and that is particularly prominent for cisgender gay men) is showing your 'camp' or 'flamboyant' side. Because of the way that society has conditioned men to think (e.g., that their self-worth and appeal is based on their masculinity), they may hide this part of their identity for fear of rejection. When we hide parts of ourselves that we really like, it can take an emotional toll and affect our wellbeing, sometimes in ways we are not even aware of. The following exercise is designed to help you think a little bit about the parts of your identity that you like and whether others see this or not. There is an example with a blank table after that you can fill in if you would like.

Table 4.1: The public and private self: examples

Things that I really like about myself that others see	Things that I really like about myself that I do not let others see	Why I do not let others see this	How could I reframe this to help me embrace it?
My friendliness Respect for others	My campness	I think others might reject me if they see my camp side. I grew up being taught that 'men should be men' and being camp does not fit with this	I recognize that this is a social narrative, and that masculinity and femininity exist on spectrums. Just because a man is camp, does not mean he is any less of a good person. I can still be friendly and respectful of others, while being camp. I do not have a problem with campness, others do! And I want to live the life I want, rather than the life other people tell me to live, or think I should live

As you can see, the example above shows that this person really likes that they are friendly and respectful, and is happy to show other people these parts of themselves. However, their campness (a way of being, behaving, speaking and acting that can be flamboyant, eccentric and downright fabulous) is not something they feel able to show others, because they grew up being told this is not how 'men' behave. In the final column, you can see that there is space for you to reframe why you do not let others see this part of your identity, if you want to fill this out. This person has done this by recognizing that this has been a story told to them by others, and that being a 'man' has nothing to do with their campness. In order to live their life the way they want to, they have considered that the problem with 'campness' actually belongs to other people: it is their problem if they do not like campness!

Of course, you may not be ready to think of ways of embracing this part of yourself, and that is completely OK. Indeed, there is something really important about safety to name here. In some instances, Queer people may not be physically, psychologically or emotionally safe to embrace parts of ourselves in public, so the extent to which you can engage with this activity may be influenced by the context you currently find yourself in. As I mentioned earlier, we do not have to let others know about every part of our identity. This exercise is useful if you really want to be able to share this with others and are finding it difficult to know where to start.

The public and private self: blank copy

Things that I really like about myself that others see	Things that I really like about myself that I do not let others see	Why I do not let others see this	How could I reframe this to help me embrace it?

BEING TRUE TO ME: LIVING MY VALUES

Something that can be tricky for some Queer people is knowing which parts of ourselves truly belong to us, and which parts of ourselves were created to please others. This is an extremely common experience for Queer people. We may have had to fit in to a family or group of people that had certain ideas and values, and if we did not do this we would be left out, or worse. If you completed the above exercise you may have already begun to think about this. Perhaps a part of your identity that you really like and did not show to others is the reason why you behaved in different ways. From the above example, behaving in an ultra-masculine and macho way is what was expected of that person, when really they wanted to embrace their campness.

A gentle way of exploring this is to think about your values. Values are beliefs, morals, principles or attitudes that help us decide how we want to live our lives. By thinking about our core values, we can consider if the situation, context or environment we are in is helping us to live by those values, or not.

In the following box is an example of some different values, to give you an idea of what a value can be.

Having fun	Making a difference	Being economical
Being free	Showing equality and fairness	Being spontaneous
Being independent	Being in control	Being independent
Keeping fit and healthy	Being happy	Caring for others
Being consistent	Having order or routine	Working hard
Being creative	Feeling like I belong	Challenging myself
Achieving things	Being faithful	Being democratic

If you want, have a go at writing out in the box below what values are important to you.

_____

_____

_____

_____

_____

_____

_____

For each value, have a go at writing out how you currently fulfil this value. If you do not do anything, then that is totally fine. You can write in the next column why you do not do anything at the moment, or what makes it tricky to keep what you currently do going. I would encourage you to think about any mental health barriers that might get in the way. For example, do you not live in line with this particular value because you feel anxious? I would also encourage you to think if any people or groups, institutions, laws or policies, or social stories get in the way. It is also OK if both of these things get in the way! Then in the final column, write down any factors that you think would need to change to help you embrace and live this value.

Here is an example, followed by a blank table for you to fill out yourself.

Table 4.2: Example table for living in line with and embracing my values

Value	How I live in line with this value *What do I do?* *How does it satisfy me?*	Why I do not live in line with this value, or what makes it difficult to do so? *Mental health-related?* *External factors?*	What would need to change?
Being kind to others	I try and empathize with others when they are struggling I always use manners	I am not always kind to myself so cannot always be kind to others Other people have taught me that who I am is wrong	I need to be kinder to myself so that I can truly be kind to others
Being independent	I make my own choices; I try not to be influenced by others	Sometimes it is hard to be independent while I still live at home	I need to move out when I can
Having fun	I go out with friends and have a laugh	If my mood is very low I do not have the motivation to meet up with people My family tell me to work hard and concentrate on getting good grades rather than having fun	I need to find ways of managing my low mood so I can meet up with friends more regularly I need to tell my parents that I can work hard AND have fun!

Blank table for living in line with and embracing my values

| Value | How I live in line with this value
What do I do?
How does it satisfy me? | Why I do not live in line with this value, or what makes it difficult to do so?
Mental health-related?
External factors? | What would need to change? |
|---|---|---|---|
| | | | |
| | | | |
| | | | |
| | | | |
| | | | |

I included the last column, *What would need to change?*, because I hope that this book will enable you to identify things that could help you to live and embrace your values more. Some of the activities here can help you to work on mental health difficulties, while also helping you think about some of the wider external factors too. It might be useful below to write out some of the things that you would like to work on to help you embrace and live your values. Space is provided below for you to do this and rate, out of 10, where you feel you are at the moment with this (with 1 being 'nowhere near where I want to be' and 10 being 'living and embracing this value'):

ACTIVITY

Figure 4.1: Keeping track of my values

Perhaps once you have worked through parts of this book you can come back and score yourself out of 10 again, and see if you have got closer to where you want to be?

SKILLS FROM OTHER SECTIONS THAT MAY BE USEFUL FOR YOU

- Skills from Chapter 8, *Feeling Anxious*

- Skills from Chapter 9, *Feeling Low*

- Skills from Chapter 5, *Self-Acceptance and Self-Compassion*
- Acceptance skills from Chapter 10, *Sleep Difficulties*

SUMMARY

- Living and embracing a Queer identity can be tricky, because of how heteronormative and cisgender society can be.
- Thinking about the context you live in can help you understand if claiming a Queer identity is easier or harder.
- There are parts of us that we may really like that we do not show to others, because perhaps we have learned to hide them.
- Working out what our personal values are, and how to live our lives in line with these, can help us to understand more about ourselves.
- Mental health difficulties and external factors may get in the way of us living our values, and there are ways we can go about changing this.

Space for your own thoughts, reflections, ideas, action plans

Chapter 5

SELF-ACCEPTANCE AND SELF-COMPASSION

WHY SELF-ACCEPTANCE CAN BE DIFFICULT FOR QUEER PEOPLE

It can be really tough growing up, living in and taking up space in a world that has been designed for the type of person that you are not, or do not want to be. From a really young age, we find that those around us – our parents, teachers, friends, family members – usually interact with and create social stories about us based on our outwardly presenting sex assigned at birth. Alongside this there is often an implicit assumption of heterosexuality. Sex education at school can exclude non-heterosexual sexuality, sexual behaviour and relationships. The pressure from peers at school to conform to heteronormative relationships is felt powerfully, and can be a huge source of anxiety and distress for Queer people. If, for example, you are assigned female at birth then the assumption is that you are comfortable with this gender identity and must be sexually attracted to men. If this social story does not fit with your internal experience of gender and/or sexuality, it can be incredibly difficult to accept this part of yourself.

People can deal with this distress in various ways:

1. Some might choose to try and ignore the 'true parts' of themselves in the hope that they will become the way that society wants or expects them to be.

2. Others may embrace their true selves, but experience bullying or rejection from people because of this.

3. Some may actively hate the parts that feel different, and fall in line with the social story that exists about Queerness. They may outwardly

speak or behave in homo/bi/transphobic ways, while feeling a huge sense of shame. This is known as *internalized homophobia*.

All these options feel like lose – lose situations don't they? Ultimately, all of these options have problematic consequences. They can lead to intense feelings such as anxiety, low mood and anger. Anger could be directed verbally or physically at yourself or others, and is an understandable emotional response. After all, why should you have to try and be someone that you are not? Why does society not just accept that some people are different? The definition of 'normal' is always shaped by those in privileged positions. These angry feelings therefore likely (and quite rightly) manifest in response to the people or groups, institutions, laws and policies and social stories that have created and maintained a heteronormative, cisgender expectation. But it can be difficult to hold this in mind when someone is calling you names. The threat of being 'outed' if you are not living as your authentic self can lead to intense activation of the 'fight or flight' response (this is our body's natural and automatic threat detection system, and I will explain this more fully in Chapter 8, *Feeling Anxious*) and maintain feelings of anxiety. The rejection experienced, or perceived, from others can really lower our mood. Basically, growing up Queer in a prejudiced world can be awful.

DID YOU KNOW?

In 1988, UK Conservative Party Prime Minister Margaret Thatcher introduced the Local Government Act. One section of this legislation – Section 28 – stated that schools and local councils could not 'promote the teaching of the acceptability of homosexuality as a pretended family relationship'. This law existed until 2003. Many teachers feared that by discussing non-heterosexual relationships and identities with school children, their jobs could be jeopardized. Homophobia from other children also often went unchallenged by teachers, because of Section 28.

Impact on mental health

Many young gay people grew up being taught in school that their identity was invalid and wrong. This was not disputed by teachers or other people in authority, leading young gay people to believe this to be true. The impact that this had on the mental health of young gay people cannot be underestimated: the direct attack on the validity of their identity by the government forced individuals to situate blame internally, rather than on this abusive policy. Self-hatred and self-punishment can lead to numerous behaviours, including self-harm, disordered eating, substance misuse and suicide attempts.

In the western world, there is a lot of emphasis on individuality and personal control and autonomy. Because of this, when something is going wrong, or we are findings things difficult, there is a tendency to look inwards

THE QUEER MENTAL HEALTH WORKBOOK

on ourselves and believe that there is something about us that must be wrong, or not functioning as it should. We do not tend to think much about the effect that external factors and influences have on us. Because of this, Queer people may struggle to accept themselves, feeling that they are existing in a world designed for others.

Before I go any further. I must emphasize one thing:

You are valid, you matter, you deserve to be here as much as anyone else and it is not your fault that the world can be a cruel place to live in.

Even though I do not know who you are reading this book, I categorically believe the above statement to be true. And I do not know if you have ever heard that said to you by someone before? If not, I want you to read it back again. And again. Perhaps you feel uneasy reading it? Or maybe you have noticed a thought such as 'that cannot be true for me' pop into your head? I want you just to notice those thoughts and feelings and read this:

The world around me has led me to believe that I should feel nervous when I assert my right to exist.

And:

The thoughts that I have in my head about myself are not always true.

I recognize that it is not as easy as just reading some statements to change how you think and feel about yourself. And accepting yourself, or being kinder to yourself, is not something that you may have felt able to, or wanted to do before. I hope that within this section you can begin to explore this concept, and experiment with how self-compassion feels if you have not been able to do this yourself yet.

RECOGNIZING WHAT HAPPENS WHEN WE STRUGGLE WITH SELF-ACCEPTANCE

Growing up Queer in a messy and unequal world can inevitably lead to some behaviours that, while at the time may have served an adaptive purpose (or continue to serve a purpose), ultimately were/are detrimental to our wellbeing. Sometimes we behave in ways that we do not always understand and engage in relationships that can feel confusing or distressing. By taking a minute to pause and recognize *why* we may do some of the things we do, we can begin to find alternative ways of behaving. For Queer people, some difficult or unhelpful behaviours may be linked to difficulties accepting their sexuality and/or gender identity. The table below identifies some things that can result from a lack of self-acceptance, with possible reasons for doing these.

Table 5.1: What struggles with self-acceptance can lead to for Queer people

What I do	Why I might do it
Difficulties with eating	To try and feel in control of at least something To punish myself
Missing school/college/university/work	To avoid others who make me feel bad for being Queer
Repeated relationships/sexual interactions with people I am not attracted to	To repress true feelings; as if doing this multiple times will 'turn me straight'
Feeling anger towards other people	To manage internalized homo/bi/transphobia; it may be easier to feel angry than low/anxious/upset
Self-injury	To regulate intense emotions To punish myself To show others that I am in pain
Suicidal thoughts	To end suffering To escape To manage feelings of rejection
Self-neglect	To punish myself – I may see 'no point' in taking care of myself
Sexual risk-taking behaviour	To feel something other than difficult emotions To punish myself
Putting myself down	The belief that if I put myself down first, then it will not hurt as much if others do this
Substance misuse (e.g., excess alcohol, illegal or prescription drugs)	To numb difficult feelings To fit in with others
Verbal or physical aggression	To feel angry instead of sad To 'get back' at people who have been mean To attack others before they attack me
Excessive video game/internet use	To escape from the 'real' world To find acceptance in other ways

Looking at the above list, it is important to recognize that all the things that we do serve a purpose. In other words, *we do it for a reason*. When accepting that living as our true selves is made difficult by the world we live in, it is unsurprising that some of the things we do may have a self-punishment function. If you wish, you can make a short list of any things that you think are unhelpful in your life, and how you think this serves a purpose for you. We will come back to these a little later:

ACTIVITY

Blank table for what struggles with self-acceptance can lead to for me

What I do	Why I might do it

SELF-COMPASSION

Self-compassion refers to the act of being kind and understanding towards ourselves, especially when we are suffering or feeling shame. A good way to introduce this concept is to start by considering the following:

- We did not choose to exist. We were created.

- We probably did not get much say in the family or environment that we grew up in.

- We did not choose to be discriminated against or abused.

- We did not choose to live in or grow up in a country that may have had or has active laws/policies against being Queer.

- If bad things happened to us, we did not choose this.

- There is a lot that we had no control over.

Yet a lot of people when they grow up, or while they are growing up, can be really harsh towards themselves. We may have perhaps even blamed ourselves for things that happened to us, or for being Queer. Practising self-compassion by being kind and gentle to ourselves, respecting ourselves, forgiving ourselves when things go wrong and recognizing that we have a right to exist and occupy space, helps us to recognize that it is OK to cut ourselves some well-deserved slack!

Our fight or flight system, designed to protect us, may have had to work overtime and may have become primed to be constantly hypervigilant and hypersensitive to any kind of threat. For some, this could lead our bodies to constantly be in high states of anxiety with thoughts racing through our heads. As you are reading this, you may feel that parts of what I have been saying resonate with you. You may have begun to feel a sense of uneasiness. It may be worth checking in with how you are feeling by scanning your body from head to toe, and noticing where you have any tension. Perhaps some of the fight or flight reset techniques from Chapter 8, *Feeling Anxious*, may be useful right now? Take a minute to pause here and go to Chapter 8 if this helps. Or, read some of the sentences above to remind yourself that perhaps you are feeling awkward or uneasy because the world never taught you to feel calm and relaxed when thinking about yourself before. It may also help to read aloud the following:

My existence is valid even if others tell me it is not.

And:

How others view me is none of my business, let them think what they want. What matters is how I view myself.

It might not seem it, but actually taking the time to check in with yourself, notice if you are feeling tense or uneasy and doing something about it is an act of self-compassion. Here are some more self-compassionate statements that may be good for you to read aloud, reflect on and think about:

It is OK to just get through the day without achieving anything in particular.

I have as much right to take up space as anybody else.

The waves will crash on the shore again tomorrow. I do not need to have everything sorted now.

Taking time to look after myself is not selfish.

Being harsh towards myself does not tend to get me anywhere, so I will try being kind to myself instead.

Why should I change the parts of myself that make me so unique?

If you want, you can use the box below to write out any of the above statements that really resonate with you. Feel free to create your own self-compassionate 'self-statements' too.

▶ ACTIVITY

ACTING COMPASSIONATELY TOWARDS THE THINGS I DO: RECOGNIZING CONTEXT

Going back to the list that you made a little earlier on, I want you to try something. I want you to notice how you described the 'function' (or the purpose) that you think this behaviour serves or served for you. I now want you to try adding a little bit more information to your description. I would like you to try adding information in such a way that a stranger could read what you have written and think to themselves: 'Well, of course they did that!' Let me show you a few examples of what I mean. The extra information I have added is in *italics*.

Table 5.2: Adding extra information to why I might do what I do

What I do	Why I might do it, *including what else has happened/is happening*
Difficulties with eating	To try and feel in control of at least something, *because I have not been able to feel in control of anything else in my life up until now*
Self-injury	To punish myself, *because the whole world seems to think something is wrong with me, so why shouldn't I?*
Excessive video game/ internet use	To escape from the 'real' world, *because the real world can be such a horrible place to have to confront every day*

If you want, give this a go below, by copying what you have written already and adding a bit more information.

ACTIVITY

Blank table for adding extra information to why I might do what I do

What I do	Why I might do it, *including what else has happened/is happening*

Now, I would like you to try one more thing. You have described a behaviour that you think is unhelpful in your life, thought about the potential function of this and now added a bit more information as to why this happens for you. When we practise self-compassion, we recognize that things that happen to and around us are not our fault. When being self-compassionate, we can begin to develop the courage to see what is in our power and gain an awareness of what is out of our control or responsibility. So, finally, I would like you to try adding one last piece of information to what you have written already. I would like you to try to be kind to yourself by writing down that you are trying your best, you are doing what you can and it is not your fault that some things are outside your control. I will provide some examples for you, following on from what I have written so far. Though remember, if this is difficult or impossible for you to do right now, that is OK. Tune into where you are at with your own wellbeing journey at the moment. You can always come back to these activities later. I will **write in bold** the self-compassionate statements. I have purposefully started each statement with 'and', because what you have written before is important and should not be dismissed:

Table 5.3: Adding a self-compassionate statement

What I do	Why I might do it, *including what else has happened/is happening*. How would a trusted friend talk to me about this? What would they say?
Difficulties with eating	To try and feel in control of at least something, *because I have not been able to feel in control of anything else in my life up until now.* **And it is not my fault that I have not been in control of other things in my life.**
Self-injury	To punish myself, *because the whole world seems to think something is wrong with me, so why shouldn't I?* **And it is not fair the whole world wants me to think that I am wrong, and it is not my fault that other people think this.**
Excessive video game/ internet use	To escape from the 'real' world, *because the real world can be such a horrible place to have to confront every day.* **And I am trying my best to be in the real world, yet feel safer on the internet.**

If you can, have a go yourself at adding a self-compassionate statement to what you have written so far. By the way, there is no right or wrong way to do this, so anything you write is going to be great. And well done for sticking with this and giving it a go!

ACTIVITY

Blank table for adding self-compassionate statements

What I do	Why I might do it, *including what else has happened/is happening.* How would a trusted friend talk to me about this? What would they say?

ACTING COMPASSIONATELY TOWARDS THE THINGS I DO: ACTING OPPOSITE

Being kind to ourselves when we are not used to doing so can feel really strange. However, cultivating kindness and compassion towards the self can be a first step in reducing any feelings of self-punishment and shame. If being kind to yourself is difficult, and you are noticing that a lot of the functions of the behaviours you are doing are about punishing yourself, then a good way to try and reduce these feelings is by 'acting opposite'. The skill of acting opposite comes from Dialectical Behaviour Therapy (DBT) (Linehan, 1993). For example, when you notice this self-punishing feeling, act by doing something that is completely opposite to this. When you may have neglected yourself by not washing or shaving, instead try make a conscious effort to have a shower/bath or shave. If you want to hurt yourself, try do something to care for yourself. If you would usually tell yourself that you are a useless person, try telling yourself that you are worth something.

Now, I realize this might sound a little strange or feel a little uncomfortable, and you might be thinking, 'Well, if it were that easy I would have done that by now'. Let me try to explain a little why doing this over a period of time can actually be quite useful. Essentially, by 'acting opposite' you are providing your brain with a brief burst of 'feel good' hormones. Because this act of self-kindness leads to some slightly more positive feelings (however small this slight change may be!), you are more likely to do it again in the future. This is usually referred to within CBT as 'behavioural activation', and I will talk about it a little more in Chapter 9, *Feeling Low*, so that you know I am not just making it up!

So even when you have feelings of being unkind to yourself, 'acting opposite' against this can have real physiological effects. You are basically training your body to expect the feeling of happy hormones when you get a self-critical or self-punishing thought or feeling. Below is a list of things you could do to 'act opposite' to feelings of self-punishment, with some space for your own ideas.

▶ ACTIVITY

Make your favourite hot/cold drink

Make your favourite meal

Do something to treat yourself (bath bomb, face mask)

Write out five things you like about yourself

Watch a feel good movie/TV show

Go for a walk/run

Read a book/magazine

_____

_____

_____

_____

_____

A good way to embed this idea into your everyday life is to create a 'feel good jar'. Get an old jam jar (or any container you have) and fill it with little bits of paper that have 'act opposite' activities on them. Keep the jar somewhere accessible, so that when you are feeling self-critical, or feel as if you want to punish yourself for some reason, you can reach into this jar and select an activity. Keep adding things to your feel good jar, and select an activity whenever you fancy it. Even better – make it part of your daily routine to do something from your feel good jar!

SELF-COMPASSION SELF-STATEMENTS

Sometimes when we are alone with only our thoughts, it can be tough to cultivate self-compassion. Giving voice to self-compassionate statements can be a powerful distraction from our thoughts. Remember the self-compassionate statements listed in Table 5.3? Some people may find it helpful to read aloud their chosen affirmations when they are feeling particularly self-critical, or when they are feeling low. Some people even like to start their day by reading aloud self-compassionate statements, as a way to centre themselves and remind them that they are valid in this world. Some people cringe at the thought of doing this, or it just does not work for them. If so, try some of the other activities in this section instead.

COMPASSIONATE LETTER WRITING

Another strategy that you can use to cultivate compassion and kindness for yourself is to write a letter, addressed to you, from you, acknowledging a difficulty or any difficulties that you are currently having. This is based on a technique developed by Irons & Beaumont (2017). This letter could be centred on one of the unhelpful things that you might have done that you have already written about above, or could be something completely different. By validating (highlighting the truthfulness of this difficulty to you) and empathizing with this struggle, you can list strategies that you have used to try and manage this. As we will explore more in Chapter 8, *Feeling Anxious*, some difficulties we have arise when our fight or flight system is activated. By gently describing how we have managed this, and what steps we could take instead when this next happens, we can reduce self-blame. Here is an example of a compassionate letter I have written to myself, to try and demonstrate the power that these letters can have.

Dear Brendan,

I am writing you this letter from a place of kindness and compassion. I know that at the moment you are trying to write this book, and writing a book can be a daunting task. It is OK to feel overwhelmed in situations like this – after all, you have never written a book before so how are you to know what to do? I know that sometimes the pressure and worry that you will not 'get things right' or that people will not like the book can activate your fight or flight system. This is perfectly understandable! Your old brain is perceiving your worry thoughts as if they were an external threat: something to hurt you. Hopefully you can find peace in the knowledge that this is just your threat system trying to keep you safe – it does not want to hurt or upset you, it is just trying to help. But this time it seems to be getting it wrong.

To cope with this, you have been working on this book quite a lot – sometimes late into the evening. Of course, you are doing this because you want everything to be perfect, because your threat system is telling you it might not be. However, I hope that you can take a step back and realize that you are trying your best and you have good intentions. Remember, it is much kinder to yourself to get a good night's sleep and wake up refreshed, rather than working late into the evenings. Perhaps you can try and set a time limit? So that after, say, 8pm you do not work on this book anymore and instead watch TV? Why don't you try that for a little while and see how it feels? And when you feel that urge to keep working late into the night, step back and tell yourself: by disconnecting from this I am actually being kind to myself and prioritizing my own self-care.

When things are feeling tricky, or self-critical thoughts start to creep back in, take the time to read this letter again, and approach these thoughts from a self-compassionate position.

With kind regards,
Brendan

I hope that in this letter you can see that I outlined the difficulty I was having (feeling overwhelmed at writing this book), validated why I was doing this (I want things to be perfect), recognized that this was resulting in my threat system becoming activated (fight or flight kicking in) and in turn I was engaging in an unhelpful behaviour (working late into the night). From there I outlined a possible step I could try to be kinder to myself (set myself a time limit so I could wind down). Compassionately committing to working towards change, rather than forcing myself to change in a self-critical and blaming way, is likely to increase the chances of me stopping at 8pm and winding down. It is a bit like when someone asks you to do something really nicely, and you think to yourself, 'Yeah, I really want to do that because they were so nice!' Compare that to when someone forces you to do something. I do not know about you but feeling forced to do things really puts me off and actually makes me want to do the complete opposite! So, by engaging with *ourselves* in a kind and gentle way, perhaps that same feeling of 'OK, yeah, I will give it a try' will resonate.

If you want to, think of a difficulty you are having at the moment. Using the compassionate letter-writing template that I have demonstrated above, write a compassionate letter to yourself in the space below. I would also encourage you to put in your letter any contextual reasons that may have contributed to your difficulty, to help you cultivate a truly compassionate and non-blaming position. For example, you may note how any systems of oppression have affected you, or how rejection from loved ones has contributed to the sensitivity of your threat system. Perhaps looking back at your circles of influence in Chapter 3, *Queer Mental Health: The Basics*, can help you with this. When you are done, read your letter back to yourself in a caring tone of voice, and notice how this feels.

ACTIVITY ▶

Dear ▼

_____

_____

_____

_____

_____

_____

_____

_____

_____

_____

_____

_____

_____

_____

_____

_____

_____

COMPASSIONATE LETTER WRITING: WRITING TO YOUR YOUNGER SELF

Some people may feel guilty because they embraced their Queer identity later on in life. Perhaps they feel as if they have missed out on some aspects of life, or feel upset that their younger self was not able to live freely for so long. Thinking about this can be hard, and one technique to manage this is to write to your younger self. In such a letter, it can be really helpful to highlight why embracing your identity earlier in life was not possible for you, what external influences were around you at the time and how this influenced this decision. And, to apologize to this part of yourself, and/or express your anger at the systemic factors that led to you not being able to fully embrace yourself, if you want to.

I once read a quote that really stuck with me. It went something like 'Shame goes to die when stories are told in safe places'. It may seem a little odd – writing a letter to yourself! – though this can be a powerfully healing activity for reducing self-blame. This is because when we hear stories of younger people who have gone through difficult experiences, our natural reaction is to empathize with their situation. We are very unlikely to blame them for what happened to them, and can usually see quite clearly how they have ended up where they are. As we have discussed previously in this chapter, it is difficult to apply this self-compassion to ourselves. However, by thinking of (and interacting with) a younger version of ourselves, we can draw on compassionate thinking much more easily.

I find it is also really helpful to highlight in the letter what parts of you are a better person because of your experiences, if you want to. There is no right or wrong way to write such a letter. In fact, many people describe the process of writing to their younger selves as quite therapeutic. It is also up to you what you do with the letter. Some people keep the letter in a safe place to read again, while others find that once they have expressed themselves on paper and read it back, they want to ceremonially burn or destroy the letter. This is all completely up to you. Here is part of an example letter to help you see what form such a letter could take:

Dear Malcolm,

Wow. What a journey it has been. As I write this letter I am 58 years old. I am living by myself, and have not married yet. Sometimes this upsets me, other times I do not mind. Maybe I will marry, maybe I will not. I am learning to find peace with this, especially because my parents always told me that they really wanted to be grandparents, and, as you know, I have not had children.

I wanted to write you this letter because there is something that I want to say to you: I am sorry. I am sorry that for so long I did not allow you to live as your true self, to be the fabulously bisexual man that you are! A lot was going on in Britain in the 1970s/1980s, and for several reasons I felt that living as my true self would have negative consequences. I am sorry yet I am also so very, very angry.

Apologizing feels weird, because keeping your true self from the world actually served a bloody good function — it kept you safe when the world around you wanted to hurt you. The world was not set up to embrace a bisexual working class man, and to be honest, I still do not think it is today. But the world is definitely a little less chaotic for you today than it was all those years ago.

The year is 2021, and you are happy today. Some days, life is tough, and you cry. What your dad told you about men crying still makes admitting this difficult. After all, men do not cry and should not show emotions. I have learned that he was not right about that though, and I cannot really blame him for that either, because that is what his parents told him. The same goes for being bisexual. He lived in a time when being anything but straight was wrong.

I tell you this now because I want you to understand that there is not one ounce of your being that is wrong. You are beautiful, you are worthy and you are a fighter. The stories that influenced your life are not the stories you need to believe, and I hope that you can continue creating new stories for yourself that are free from the grip that shame and stigma had on you for so many years.

You can write a letter to a younger self at any age. Of course, you do not have to write to yourself about embracing your Queer identity later on. You may want to write a letter to a younger self who experiences difficulties, such as bullying, abuse, discrimination or rejection. Here is a space for you to write a letter to your younger self, if you want to.

ACTIVITY

Dear

_____

_____

_____

_____

_____

_____

_____

_____

_____

_____

_____

_____

SYSTEMIC SELF-COMPASSION

From an individualist perspective, self-compassion is often based on the idea that the thoughts and feelings we experience can be unhelpful, and that we as individuals can connect to these in a different way, through kindness. What can sometimes go amiss in this pursuit, I think, is the focus on external factors, people and contexts that can be contributing to difficulties. For example, a young Queer person may be living with emotionally abusive parents who invalidate their identity. While the strategies described above may be helpful to externalize this abuse as belonging outside the person, this does not remove the source of the problem: the emotionally abusive parents. The most self-compassionate thing for this young Queer person to do in this situation is to distance themselves from this negativity and abuse, by perhaps moving in with other family/friends or going to live by themselves.

With the above example, I am under no illusion that simply 'moving out' is an easy and viable option. I am acutely aware that this is potentially a luxury not available to many, and that our relationships with our parents may be complex and not always completely negative. What I hope to be able to demonstrate in the above example is that recognizing that the source of the problem is external to ourselves (that it is something else, not us!) can be the first step in bringing about change, and can be an act of self-compassion. Perhaps this young person can have a conversation with their parents, or ask a friend to come along while they have this conversation, if they feel unable to do it alone. Perhaps they can reach out to a charity or a peer support group or service that can help them problem-solve the situation. Sometimes, by putting your interests ahead of other people, you are being kind to yourself.

Another way of being systemically self-compassionate is by seeking out people in your life who uplift you, nourish you and bring joy into your life. Sometimes this is referred to as 'finding your tribe' or 'finding your people'. People can do this in different ways: through youth groups, school/college/ university, online communities, Queer spaces and through shared interests (sports, cosplay, video games, drag etc.). Allowing yourself to feel connected to others can be a liberating and compelling act of self-compassion.

SUMMARY

- The world we live in, and our experiences growing up, can make accepting our Queer identity difficult.

- We can internalize homo/bi/transphobia, and this can take the form of unhelpful behaviours (such as self-harm, eating difficulties or excessive alcohol use).

- We can practise self-compassion by thinking about the purpose of these behaviours within context and by 'acting opposite' to feelings of self-punishment.

- Writing a compassionate letter to ourselves can be a good tool to use to help us externalize any difficulties we may be blaming ourselves for.

- Sometimes self-compassion is about thinking about the people or things in our life that negatively impact on our wellbeing, and doing something about this.

Space for your own thoughts, reflections, ideas, action plans

— Chapter 6 —

QUEER RELATIONSHIPS

Dr Brendan J Dunlop and Dr James Lea

Relationships are an integral part of what it means to be human, as we are social animals. As mentioned before, very few of us live on remote abandoned islands, and so we constantly live our lives in relation to other people and things. Even if we did live on a remote island, we would still have a relationship with ourselves (e.g., things we like or do not like about ourselves, or the thoughts and feelings we have).

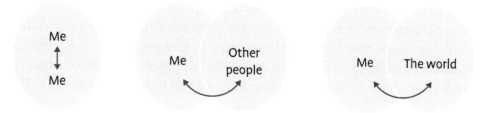

Figure 6.1: We can have relationships with ourselves, with others and with the wider world

TYPES OF RELATIONSHIPS

When we think of relationships, most people probably think of relationships between two or more people. The relationship we have with ourselves is also very important, and hopefully within Chapter 4, *Identity*, and Chapter 5, *Self-Acceptance and Self-Compassion*, you have been able to think about the relationship that you have with yourself. We can also have relationships with the wider world. For example, this could be a relationship with a particular institution, with our work or education, with religion or faith, or with the Queer community.

While holding in mind that we can have relationships with the wider world and with ourselves, in this chapter I would like particularly to introduce three broad kinds of relationships for you to think about and consider in your life:

- Emotionally and/or sexually intimate relationships, for example sexual, romantic, companionship.

- Family relationships and friendships, for example birth family relationships, chosen family or 'logical family' (Maupin, 2017), close and important friends.

- Other social relationships, for example work colleagues, acquaintances, community members, local services, neighbourhood.

I hope to be able to help you identify which types of relationships you might have in your life already, what you get from these relationships and whether there are relationships that you would like to develop or distance yourself from.

HOW TO SPEAK WITH OTHERS AND DEVELOP MORE RELATIONSHIPS

Before I discuss more about the different types of relationships we can have, I am very aware that for a variety of reasons, making friends and forming relationships with others can be tricky for Queer people. This will be explored a little more later on in this chapter. Perhaps you have been rejected in the past when you have tried to make connections with others? Or, the world or other people have led you to believe that no one wants to be in a relationship with you? Even if this is not the case, sometimes we can all feel lonely and wish we had more connections and relationships in our lives. We human beings can often worry about what others think of us, which can get in the way of us talking to new people or trying to make new connections. Are you the kind of person who often gets nervous talking to new people? If so, then I would like to introduce a technique that might help you. It comes from Dialectical Behaviour Therapy (Linehan, 1993, 2015; Rathus & Miller, 2015) and is designed to help us in these situations. It is called the THINK skill. THINK stands for: *Think, Have empathy, Interpretations, Notice* and *use Kindness.*

We can all have different ideas about what we think is happening in social situations. We can often act as though these judgements and interpretations are facts and are true (it is a shame that most of the time they are not). So, the first question to ask yourself is: what assumptions am I making about myself or the other person? For example, you might think that a particular person looked cross when you smiled at them. The next question to ask yourself is: what does that assumption make me feel and do? For example, you might feel embarrassed, which stops you from smiling again, or going over to say hello.

Let us apply the THINK skill to see if we can approach and think about the situation differently:

Table 6.1: Applying the THINK skill to relationships

	Applying the skill	**Thinking about the situation differently**
Think	Think about the situation from the other person's perspective	The other person did not see me smiling. They were looking at their phone
Have empathy	What might the other person be feeling or thinking?	They may have got some bad news They may be bored
Interpretations	What are the other interpretations or explanations for what I think is happening?	They might be upset They maybe just pulled a face that did not mean anything (maybe that is just how their face looks?!)
Notice	Notice what the other person is actually communicating with their face, body, words	They seem nervous; maybe they are feeling uncomfortable in this situation?
use Kindness	Can you use kindness with yourself and the other person? Can you try and be gentle with yourself?	Maybe I can be kind to them and go and say hello. Maybe I can be gentle with myself, reminding myself I am a pretty cool person!

(copyright Dr Brendan J Dunlop & Dr James Lea 2021)

So, if you want to try this skill out for yourself when you are next thinking about creating connections with others, or are having some difficulties doing so, first think to yourself:

What assumptions am I making about myself or the other person?

What does that assumption make me feel and do?

On the following page is a blank table to fill in and practise the THINK skill, if you like.

ACTIVITY

 Blank THINK skill table

	Applying the skill	Thinking about the situation differently
Think	Think about the situation from the other person's perspective	
Have empathy	What might the other person be feeling or thinking?	
Interpretations	What are the other interpretations or explanations for what I think is happening?	
Notice	Notice what the other person is actually communicating with their face, body, words	
use Kindness	Can you use kindness with yourself and the other person? Can you try and be gentle with yourself?	

(copyright Dr Brendan J Dunlop & Dr James Lea 2021)

Practise using this skill and it is hoped that, over time, it will feel easier to speak with new people. This is because you will be less likely to believe the stories you tell yourself, or that your mind tries to tell you, and have more chance of making connections and future friendships.

RELATIONSHIPS IN CONTEXT: CIRCLES OF CLOSENESS

You may notice that some of the relationships I have described above align with the circles of influence introduced in the previous chapter. If you completed this previous exercise, you may have already made links between these external influences and yourself. These links could be important relationships that are affecting your mental health and wellbeing in good or not so good ways.

To help you think more specifically about the relationships in your life, I would like to introduce a new set of circles – the 'circles of closeness'. This set of circles can help you think specifically about relationships that you have with other people, and how close this relationship feels for you. Let us demonstrate with an example:

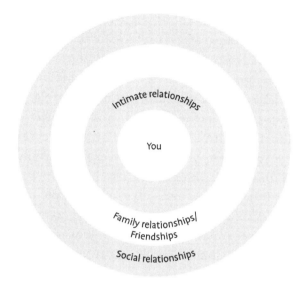

Figure 6.2: Circles of closeness (copyright Dr Brendan J Dunlop & Dr James Lea 2021)

Figure 6.3: Example circles of closeness: Tilda (copyright Dr Brendan J Dunlop & Dr James Lea 2021)

From the above circles of closeness, we can see that Tilda has three people who are sexually and emotionally intimate relations of hers – her partners Cassandra and William, and her best friend Milly. For family and friends, Tilda has her mum, dad and step-mum. In her social relationships circle she has her best work friend, the people she talks to at the gym and the friends she has made at a lesbian and bisexual women's support group.

It is also helpful to think about what exactly Tilda gets from these relationships. This is because we can get lots of different needs met within relationships, such as *practical needs* (e.g., shelter, food, money); *emotional needs* (e.g., love, belonging, respect); *sexual needs* (psychological and physical desire); *social connection needs* and *participation needs* (e.g., shared interests, support groups clubs, local neighbourhood); and *exchange/service needs* (paid or unpaid relationships with a doctor, dentist, hairdresser, mental health professional etc.). Wherever, or from whoever, you get these needs met is totally fine. Thinking about who meets these needs for you could be really helpful, especially if there is a particular person or people who seem to satisfy a lot of needs, or particular individuals who actually do not meet any (or only very few) needs for you. We can do this by thinking about the relationships Tilda has and identifying what she is getting from each one:

Table 6.2: Relationships in Tilda's life, and what she gets from them

Person	Closeness	What I get
Cassandra	Intimate	Sexual (psychological and physical desire) needs met
William	Intimate	Sexual (psychological and physical desire) and emotional (love, belonging and respect) needs met
Best friend Milly	Intimate	Emotional needs (love, belonging, respect)
Mum	Family	Nothing
Dad	Family	Practical (financial and housing) needs met
Step-mum	Family	Practical (financial and housing) and emotional (love, belonging and respect) needs met
Work best friend	Social	Social and emotional needs (connection, belonging, joy)
Friends from lesbian and bi+ support group	Social	Social and emotional needs (connection, belonging, psychological safety)
People at the gym	Social	Social needs (connection, belonging)

(copyright Dr Brendan J Dunlop & Dr James Lea 2021)

Looking at what Tilda actually gets from these relationships, it is clear that relationships with different people meet different needs. It is also evident that one particular relationship – her relationship with her mum – does not seem to meet any needs, despite this being a relationship quite close to Tilda. On the other hand, Tilda's work best friend seems to meet both her social and emotional needs, and her step-mum meets her practical and emotional needs. The reason this could be a helpful exercise is that it can help to identify if there are relationships that we may be investing a lot of time, effort, or resources in, and actually getting very little back. It also allows us to recognize those relationships that might not feel very close to us at the moment, but when we zoom out and think about what we get from them, they are actually really key relationships that it might be worth investing more time or energy in. If Tilda is investing a lot of time and effort in her relationship with her mum, and is not getting anything back from this, this could be detrimental for Tilda's mental health and wellbeing. Perhaps Tilda having an honest conversation with her mum and stating that she does not feel as if she is getting anything from their relationship could be a catalyst for change. Alternatively, if Tilda does this and her mum is not willing to make any kind of effort, perhaps it may be beneficial for Tilda to concentrate on the other more fulfilling relationships in her life, such as the relationship with her work best friend. This can be quite painful to think about, especially when we come to realize that some relationships in our lives are not doing anything for us, even though we think highly of the people concerned. This is a difficult situation to be aware of, though I promise you that in the long run it is better to know, so you can create relationships that meet your needs with people you like. So please go easy on yourself as you complete this activity.

On the following pages there is a blank copy of the circles of closeness and a blank table for you to write out what you get from each relationship, if you like:

ACTIVITY

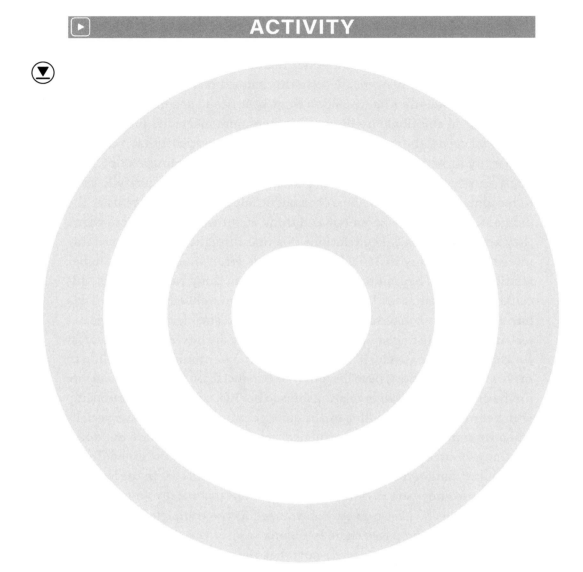

*Figure 6.4: Blank circles of closeness (copyright Dr
Brendan J Dunlop & Dr James Lea 2021)*

ACTIVITY

Blank table for the relationships in your life, and what you get from them

Person	Closeness	What I get

(copyright Dr Brendan J Dunlop & Dr James Lea 2021)

Because relationships are so key to our everyday lives, when we experience difficulties in relationships, this can affect our mental health and wellbeing. For example, if you have an argument with your friend or partner, you may feel anxious or low in mood afterwards. Your relationship with yourself, or certain parts of yourself, can be affected by things that may have happened to you. If you have experienced trauma, you may doubt your ability to keep yourself safe (despite the fact that it was not your fault), and therefore experience intense emotions that are difficult to manage.

RELATIONSHIPS: WHY THEY MIGHT
BE TRICKY FOR QUEER PEOPLE

Queer relationships can often look and feel different to typical cishet relationships.

Relationships for Queer people may have been confusing because some Queer people felt they had to hide parts of themselves for others to like them or want to be close to them. Some people call this a 'conditional relationship', as we get or do not get the things we want based on what we agree to do or not do. Take, for example, a friendship at school. A young Queer person may have been told by their peers that they will only be friends with them *if they do not act gay*. Or a parental relationship, where parents may tell their child that they will only love them if they *do not tell anyone that they are Queer*. Indeed, relationships with religion may also be conditional: *Jesus/ Allah will only love you if you repent for your sins*. Being in a relationship that is *not* conditional on anything else can therefore understandably sometimes feel strange for some Queer people. It can feel super weird for someone to like you, just for you, without you needing to hide parts of yourself, or feel ashamed for being who you are!

Relationships may also be abusive. If someone found out that you were Queer, they may have taken advantage of your vulnerability, especially if you are/were questioning your identity. They may have acted as if they were friendly and understanding, but they may have had an ulterior motive (e.g., sex, money, accommodation etc.). Family may have tried to 'cure' your Queerness by suggesting 'conversion therapy', prayer or other things. This can be really, really difficult to comprehend – that people who are supposed to love you no matter what, are telling you part of your very being is 'wrong' and needs 'fixing' (it absolutely *does not*, by the way). Because of this, being able to trust people can be difficult. You may always have in the back of your mind *'Will they abandon me?'* or *'What if they use my Queerness against me?'*

If you have lived your life having to censor yourself in relationships, or have experienced abuse or manipulation within relationships, then the boundaries and safety of this type of connection can be confusing. This can mean that some Queer people in relationships can have specific ideas about what relationships should be or should not be, and so quite understandably can fall into unhelpful or harmful patterns, such as:

- staying in unhealthy or abusive relationships, because this feels normal or familiar as you can predict what will happen

- attaching to someone else very quickly and seeming quite intense, because relationships have always been all or nothing and you feel as though you need to prove how into them you are

- not ever attaching to someone else, because if you do, you think you may get hurt, so it is better to keep yourself to yourself

- not knowing how to say no, for example when it comes to sex, because you always put other people's needs and desires before your own

- being drawn to relationships where you will inevitably be exploited, financially, sexually or emotionally, because this feels normal and familiar to what you have previously known

- being stand-offish or hostile when others try to form a connection, because it is easier to push people away than trust them and potentially get hurt

- always believing that other people must be right, because you have always been told that you are wrong.

Relationship difficulties or unhelpful patterns can cause us psychological distress, and in turn contribute to mental health difficulties or poorer psychological wellbeing. To illustrate how these things can be connected, let us use the example patterns above. As you can see in the table below, we will describe how these types of patterns could lead to mental health difficulties for some people:

Table 6.3: Potential mental health and wellbeing consequences for unhelpful relationship patterns

Relationship pattern	Potential consequences for mental health and psychological wellbeing
Staying in unhealthy or abusive relationships, because this feels normal or comfortable as you can predict what will happen	Physical, psychological, emotional or sexual abuse; low self-esteem/confidence; feeling low in mood; feeling anxious; feeling shame; feeling scared; feeling angry; feeling lonely

cont.

Relationship pattern	Potential consequences for mental health and psychological wellbeing
Attaching to someone else very quickly and being quite intense, because relationships have always been all or nothing and you feel as though you need to prove how into them you are	Feeling anxious; constantly worrying; emotional and physical exhaustion
Not ever attaching to someone else, because if you do, you think you may get hurt, so it is better to keep yourself to yourself	Feeling low in mood; feeling lonely; feeling angry
Not knowing how to say no, for example when it comes to sex, because you put other people's needs and desires before your own	Physical, psychological, emotional or sexual abuse; not getting own needs met; low self-esteem/confidence; feeling low in mood; feeling anxious; feeling shame; feeling scared; feeling angry; feeling lonely
Being drawn to relationships where you will inevitably be exploited, financially, sexually or emotionally, because this feels normal and comfortable, because you can predict what will happen	Physical, psychological, emotional or sexual abuse; low self-esteem/confidence; feeling low in mood; feeling anxious; feeling shame; feeling scared; feeling angry; feeling lonely
Being stand-offish or hostile when others try to form a connection, because it is easier to push people away than trust them and potentially get hurt	Feeling angry; feeling low in mood; feeling anxious; feeling lonely
Always believing that other people must be right, because you have always been told that you are wrong	Low self-esteem/confidence; not getting own needs met; constantly doubting yourself

(copyright Dr Brendan J Dunlop & Dr James Lea 2021)

Perhaps it might be helpful to see if any of the above relationship patterns are present in your life? The wording I have used above might not quite fit for you, so feel free to change the words so it makes sense. It should also be said that this is not a prescriptive list of potential consequences to come from these patterns. You may experience some, all or none of them. So, again, just change the wording or write down whatever is most relevant for you.

ACTIVITY

Blank table for potential relationship patterns,
and consequences of these, in your life

Relationship pattern	Potential consequences for mental health and psychological wellbeing

(copyright Dr Brendan J Dunlop & Dr James Lea 2021)

RELATIONSHIP DIVERSITIES

Queer identities and relationships can often look and feel different from typical or normative cishet relationships. Dominic Davies said that as a Queer community 'We include people on the aromantic (aro) spectrum...people with multipartnered relationships (swingers, non-monogamous, polyamorous people) as well as those in "monogamish" forms of partnerships' (Pink Therapy, 2021). For example, aromantic people may feel sexual attraction to others, but they do not necessarily develop romantic connections. For asexual people, they may romantically connect with another person/people, without the feelings or urges to engage in sexual activity. For people who are polyamorous, they may develop intimate relationships with more than one partner. People in 'open relationships' may have one romantic partner with whom they are in a relationship, and engage in sexual activity with others while part of this. Polyamorous and open relationships are not necessarily unique to Queer people though this type of relationship diversity can be common within the LGBTQ+ community.

Relationship diversity challenges the heteronormative status quo. While Queer people and Queer relationships have always existed, the dominant social story for romance is that of a cisgender man being in a monogamous relationship with a cisgender woman, who have their own birth children. Policy and laws have focused on this type of relationship as the best or only type of relationship; religious institutions have often cited religious texts as 'supporting' this notion; and, consequently, traditional marriage (and the legal protections and rights that come with this) emphasizes this. This type of relationship is therefore taught in school as 'normal', and what people should be aiming for in their lives. Consequently, people and groups grow up believing that anything different from this 'normal' relationship is wrong, sinful, weird or any other judgemental adjective you can think of. This can have huge implications for Queer people. Self-esteem and mood can be affected, feelings of shame can creep in and some people may hurt themselves to manage such feelings. It is probably worth spelling out the following:

Relationships should only matter to the people within them. Your relationships are not immoral or wrong.

Remember the visual cycle of oppression I introduced in Chapter 3, *Queer Mental Health: The Basics?* This is very applicable when it comes to relationships. Cishet people are not always invested in embracing relationship diversity, because *people like what they know and they like to feel comfortable.* The default position when something different comes along is to shut this down, as this reduces the feelings of anxiety that accompany facing something different. In other words, people often make others feel bad for the differences in their relationship not because there is anything inherently wrong with it, but *because it makes others feel uncomfortable, confused and makes them question their own relationship choices.* This feels really important to write down and communicate to you, because I think understanding this can sometimes take the sting out of any feelings of anxiety, low mood or shame that people might be feeling.

MAKING RELATIONSHIPS WORK FOR YOU

So, we have established that there are different types of relationships we can experience in our lives and that we can get our needs met by different people.

Queer relationships can be trickier than cishet relationships because previous experiences may have led to ideas about what relationships need to be or should be, creating unhelpful or unhealthy patterns. Such patterns mean that we may not get some of our core needs met by such relationships, and they may actually adversely impact our wellbeing. Recognizing which relationships in our lives are not doing anything for us, or are detrimental to our mental health and wellbeing, is the first step to being able to do something about this.

SKILLS FROM OTHER SECTIONS THAT MAY BE USEFUL FOR YOU

- Skills from Chapter 4, *Identity*

- Skills from Chapter 5, *Self-Acceptance and Self-Compassion*

- Skills from Chapter 8, *Feeling Anxious*

- Skills from Chapter 9, *Feeling Low*

SUMMARY

- We exist in relation to other people, and sometimes it can be tricky to know how to make friends and form relationships.

- Different people and different relationships in our life can give us different things, and it can be helpful to recognize what we get from these relationships.

- For some Queer people, relationships have often been conditional, and based on the understanding that the Queer person must do something, or censor a part of themselves, for the relationship to work.

- Because relationships for some Queer people have been conditional on other things, this means they can feel tricky to navigate, leading to patterns that are unhelpful and can cause mental health difficulties.

- There is a broad spectrum of relationship diversities within the Queer community, and just because this can challenge heteronormative assumptions and traditions, does not mean that such relationships are wrong!

Space for your own thoughts, reflections, ideas, action plans

Chapter 7

INTERSECTIONALITY AND ME

Dr Brendan J Dunlop and Dr James Lea

WHAT IS INTERSECTIONALITY?

At this point in the book, I hope you are beginning to get a better sense of you, what you need, and what you can do to create and maintain your well-being and the life you want to live. I thought that this may be a good time to help you think about something called 'intersectionality' and why it might be useful for Queer people to know about in relation to our identity, distress and wellbeing. In this chapter, I will introduce some key ideas and things for you to think about in relation to intersectionality. Towards the end, I will bring these together to create an 'intersectional person' – or, more specifically, an 'intersectional *you*' that can help you to reflect on and understand the different parts of your identity.

Intersectionality is a long word used to describe a pretty simple (and useful) idea. To understand it, let us start with a question. Apart from iden-tifying as Queer, can you list three other aspects of you and your identity that you think are important? For example, this could be your race/ethnicity/ethnic origin, any disabilities you may have or your culture.

ACTIVITY ▶

1. _____

2. _____

3. _____

So, I hope that you will agree that there are various aspects of you and your identity that make you complex and interesting, apart from just being Queer. This is important to the idea of intersectionality. In fact, it was the reason that the word and the theory was created by Kimberlé Crenshaw (1989), in her attempt to understand how American law could respond to issues where gender and race discrimination were happening at the same time.

In essence, intersectionality is interested in trying to understand the following questions:

- What characteristics and identities do we hold, and what groups could we belong to?

- What role do power, privilege and inequality play in relation to these identities?

- How do these characteristics and distinct discriminations interact and create new, more complex, forms of discrimination, and therefore distress for the same person?

Intersectionality uses a metaphor of cars and roads to explain a complex idea. As a reference point for this metaphor, let us picture a white, straight, able-bodied cisgender man who has never had to even step out into the road because of the privileged position this type of person holds within society. They are safe: they do not need to go anywhere or do anything because society accepts them for who they are.

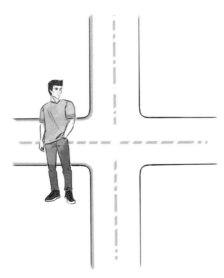

Figure 7.1: Staying safe: no cars to dodge

EXAMPLE: DELSIERENE

Here, Delsierene, a woman who is African American, is standing in the middle of the crossroads (Americans call this an 'intersection', hence the term 'intersectionality').

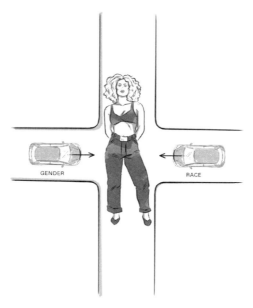

Figure 7.2: Dodging cars: the intersection of race and gender

Delsierene has cars coming from two directions, meaning she has multiple cars to dodge, otherwise she will get hurt.

- She has to be vigilant about the cars.

- She has to use more energy trying to miss the cars.

- She has to spend more energy to keep herself safe.

In this example, understanding the intersectionality of Delsierene could look like this:

- Characteristics, identities and groups: woman and Black (non-man and non-white).

- Power and inequality: Delsierene experiences less power and privilege being a woman; and experiences less power and privilege being Black.

There is dual inequality and discrimination for these aspects of her identity.

- Racism, sexism and misogyny are directed at Delsierene.

Based on our understanding of Delsierene and intersectionality:

- How do you think Delsierene feels in her day-to-day life?

- What is her experience of oppression and discrimination?

- Do you think she feels exhausted and distressed by her experience in the world?

- Do you think she feels frustrated at institutions and services for not understanding all aspects of her at the same time, for example health, education, social services?

Use the box below to write down any thoughts, ideas or reflections that you have based on these questions and the 'intersectional understanding' we have developed about Delsierene.

ACTIVITY

_____

_____

_____

_____

_____

_____

EXAMPLE: HAWKE

Here, Hawke is standing in the middle of the crossroads/intersection. Hawke is a non-binary person who is Indian. Hawke was born deaf, and identifies as culturally Deaf with British Sign Language (BSL) being their first language. Hawke identifies as pansexual.

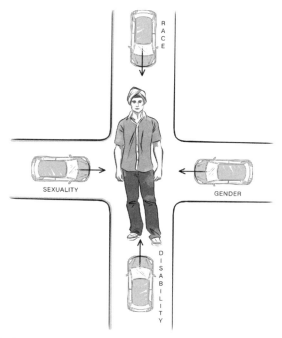

Figure 7.3: Dodging cars: the intersection of race, gender, sexuality and disability

Hawke has cars coming from four directions, meaning they have lots of cars to dodge, otherwise they will get hurt.

- Hawke has to be hypervigilant about the cars.

- Hawke has to use huge amounts of energy trying to miss the cars.

- Hawke has to spend huge amounts of energy to keep themself safe.

In our example, understanding the intersectionality of Hawke could look like this:

- Characteristics, identities and groups: non-binary (gender: non-cis-gendered); Indian (race: non-white); Deaf and first language BSL (disability: non-hearing); and pan (sexuality: non-heterosexual).

- Power and inequality: Hawke experiences less power and privilege being non-binary; experiences less power and privilege being Indian; experiences less power and privilege being Deaf; experiences less power and privilege using a non-English language; and experiences less power and privilege being pansexual. There are multiple inequalities and discriminations for these aspects of their identity.

- Cisgenderism, transphobia, racism, ableism, language bias, homo/biphobia are directed at Hawke.

Based on our understanding of Hawke and intersectionality:

- How do you think Hawke feels in their day-to-day life?

- What is their experience of oppression and discrimination?

- Do you think Hawke feels exhausted and distressed by their experience in the world?

- Do you think they feel frustrated at institutions and services for not understanding all the aspects of them at the same time, for example health, education, social services?

Just as you might have done with Delsierene, use the box below to write down any thoughts, ideas or reflections that you have based on these questions and the 'intersectional understanding' we have developed about Hawke.

ACTIVITY

_____

_____

_____

_____

_____

_____

CIRCLES OF POWER AND PRIVILEGE

People like Delsierene and Hawke are more likely to experience complex forms of discrimination, psychological distress and mental health difficulties because of their multiple intersecting minority group identities.

This is because all characteristics and identities are associated with power and privilege in society. Such power and privilege stem from the stories and narratives that exist about certain identities, and how these privileged identities are given precedence and value. Unfortunately, minoritized identities and characteristics, like the ones we have, are often associated with less power and privilege in society. This does not just happen! Particular stories about which identities or characteristics are 'desirable' have historical links to genocide (the attempts to exterminate a certain race or ethnic group), eugenics (the practice of excluding so-called 'inferior' genes from being passed on) and divisions between social classes. So, the idea that one characteristic is 'better' than another is a complete story, and usually a story written by people in positions of influence, in a bid to maintain their power.

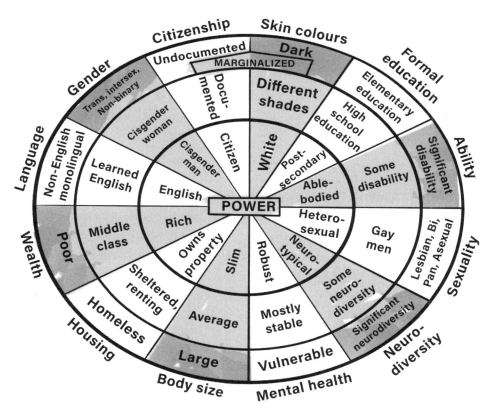

Figure 7.4: Wheel of power and privilege

Take a look at the diagram on the previous page. As you can see, there are people in the world, including Queer people, who have less power and privilege in society just because of who they are. We could basically say that parts of their power and privilege are taken away from them simply because of the stories that exist about their minoritized characteristics and identities. The more minoritized characteristics and identities a person holds, the more power and privilege is taken away from them. As you can imagine, this can make people feel misunderstood, frustrated, sad and alone (as well as lots of other difficult emotions). This is what intersectionality can help us to understand about our own experience of the world, and the experience of others.

Audre Lorde is an important figure in the world of intersectionality. She self-identified as a Black, lesbian, mother, warrior and poet. She dedicated her life and creativity to confronting injustices of racism, sexism, classism, heterosexism and homophobia. She believed that 'there is no such thing as a single-issue struggle, as we do not lead single-issue lives' (Lorde, 1984, p.147).

It is good to put some real voices to what has been introduced to you in the first part of this chapter. To do this, you could watch this video of Queer people from Glasgow talking about their identities and experience in the world from an intersectional perspective (Equality Network, 2016): www.youtube.com/watch?v=yqTCAuj78ac.

UNDERSTANDING MY OWN INTERSECTIONALITY

I hope you are now beginning to understand intersectionality and know how it can be helpful for understanding ourselves as Queer people in the world. This next section will focus on you trying to understand your own intersectionality and how this relates to psychological wellbeing and mental health.

Here is a list of identities and characteristics to help us label and understand aspects of our identity to get a better understanding of ourselves and why we might struggle in the world sometimes. Within the UK, some of these characteristics are called *protected characteristics*, which means it is against the law to discriminate against someone because of these aspects of their identity, under the Equality Act (2010).

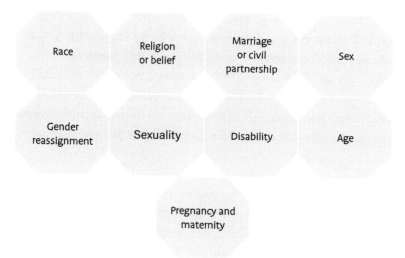

Figure 7.5: Protected Characteristics (Equality Act, 2010)

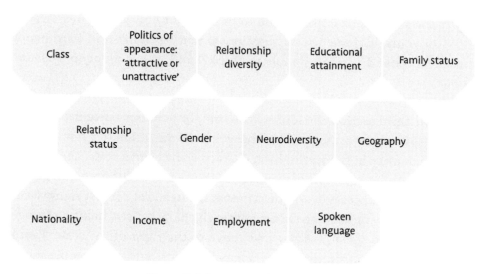

Figure 7.6: Important characteristics

ACTIVITY

Using the characteristics from the lists above, and your own ideas, move to the 'intersectional person' worksheet on the next few pages to get a better understanding of what characteristics and identities you hold, and how you express these aspects of yourself; what roles power, privilege and inequality play in relation to these identities; and how these characteristics and distinct discriminations interact and create new complex forms of discrimination and potential stress for you. There is a completed example to guide you, and then a blank worksheet for you to complete, if you want to.

The purpose of the intersectional person worksheet is to help increase your awareness and understanding of yourself as an intersectional human being. Learning about yourself in this way will help you understand aspects of your life that cause you difficulties, hopefully helping you see how to move forward.

1 The first box is simply asking you to make a list of the things that make you who you are in the world. It is important to think about the aspects of you that are obvious to other people (visible), as well as the characteristics of you that are not easy to know or see (not visible). It might be helpful to look back at the wheel of power and privilege to help with this.

2 The second box is asking you to think about how you express aspects of yourself. Some useful questions might be 'What do I want people to see?', 'What do I want people to think?' and 'What do people assume about me?'

3 The third section can look a little complicated, but I promise it is not. It is basically asking you to label yourself in relation to a few different areas of identity in the world. Each characteristic is on a scale: the left side is linked with less power and privilege in the world, and therefore a greater experience of oppression and discrimination in society (most minoritized identities). The middle line shows how each characteristic holds a stronger value of being a social 'norm' as we move to the right of the scale. People often say these characteristics are 'normal', 'typical' and what people should be. The right side of the scale is linked with more power and privilege in society, and far less experience of oppression and discrimination. You can put a cross on each of the scales where you think you are. You can then link the dots and get a visual idea of what aspects of your intersectional identity are associated with more or less power, privilege, oppression and discrimination. It is important to note that this is not an exact science. It is simply meant to provide you with a visual representation that can help you to think about the aspects of you that may make it easier for you to move freely about in the world, and aspects of your identity that may make it more difficult for you, due to institutional oppression. Another important point is that this question does not intend to invalidate anyone's particular identity. For instance, for race, on the example scale I give there is 'white' on the right side, and then 'Person of Colour, BAME, Indigenous or First Nation' on the left. If you place a mark in the middle of this line, this does not necessarily mean you identify as mixed race or mixed heritage. It could, but it does not have to mean that. I intend for it to instead allow for a visual representation of the influence of power that comes with marginalized groups, and the fact that the closer you place a mark towards the 'white' end of the scale, the more power and privilege you think your particular race has in a world that tends to place value on 'whiteness'.

4 The fourth box is asking you to think about times and places when you maximize or minimize aspects of yourself, and what kinds of people you do this with. Ask yourself 'Why do I do this?' and 'Does it keep me safe?'

5 The fifth box is asking you questions to help you think about how your own intersectionality can link to your experience of distress and mental health difficulties, and how those feelings may link to oppression and discrimination in the world. It may be good to look back at the cycle of oppression (Chapter 3, *Queer Mental Health: The Basics*) to help you with this.

6 The sixth box encourages you to be authentically honest with yourself about what you would like, and what you might need to change to get those things. This also includes in what ways, and how, you can be gentler with yourself and take care of yourself in the world.

Let us demonstrate with the example of 'Gwi', so that you can see how to complete this activity. It should be noted that some of the characteristics and identities that Gwi identifies with (e.g., 'Aspie') are based on their own choice of language. For example, not everyone who is neurodivergent will identify with or use such terms.

THE INTERSECTIONAL PERSON: CREATING AN 'INTERSECTIONAL ME' WORKSHEET EXAMPLE

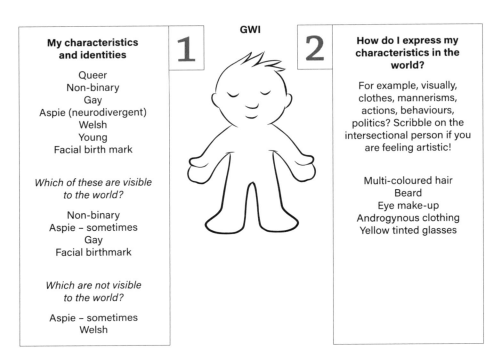

GWI

1

My characteristics and identities

Queer
Non-binary
Gay
Aspie (neurodivergent)
Welsh
Young
Facial birth mark

Which of these are visible to the world?

Non-binary
Aspie – sometimes
Gay
Facial birthmark

Which are not visible to the world?

Aspie – sometimes
Welsh

2

How do I express my characteristics in the world?

For example, visually, clothes, mannerisms, actions, behaviours, politics? Scribble on the intersectional person if you are feeling artistic!

Multi-coloured hair
Beard
Eye make-up
Androgynous clothing
Yellow tinted glasses

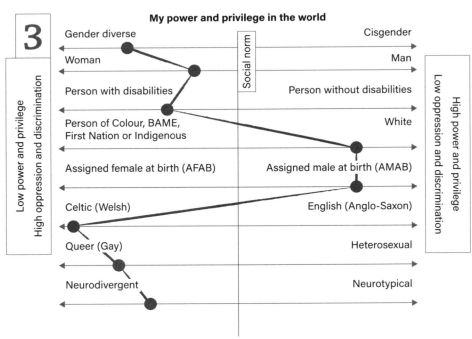

My power and privilege in the world

3

Low power and privilege
High oppression and discrimination

High power and privilege
Low oppression and discrimination

Social norm

Gender diverse — Cisgender

Woman — Man

Person with disabilities — Person without disabilities

Person of Colour, BAME, First Nation or Indigenous — White

Assigned female at birth (AFAB) — Assigned male at birth (AMAB)

Celtic (Welsh) — English (Anglo-Saxon)

Queer (Gay) — Heterosexual

Neurodivergent — Neurotypical

4 Imagine a volume button that you can turn up or turn down. In what places, and with whom, do I 'turn the volume up' on aspects of my identity?

For example, do I allow myself to inhabit my Queer identity more when I am with other Queer people?

I deffo allow myself to turn up my queerness and my aspie ways when I am with other queer people — friends. I am more Welsh and speak Welsh when I am at home with my family, so I turn up these parts of me then.

In what places, and with whom, do I 'turn the volume down' on aspects of my identity?

For example, do I feel less able to inhabit my British Pakistani or African American identity when I am with white people?

I turn down my Welshness around English people.
I turn down my neurodivergent self when I am at work.
I turn down being non-binary in the world, and will respond to male pronouns.

In what places, and with whom, can I just leave 'leave the volume button wherever it is' and feel most comfortable being my intersectional self?

With my best friend, Ronnie; with my dog, Jasper; with my partner Jacks.

5 Questions that might take more time to think about:

How do I feel in my day-to-day life?

I often feel as though I do not quite fit in completely in many places — it can feel lonely being me. I often feel sad and anxious about who or what I have to be around others.

What power and inequality do I experience in the world as a result of my intersectional identity?

I experience less power and privilege being non-binary (slight leaning towards woman as a gender); being gay; being seen as disabled by being neurodivergent; being Welsh. I experience more power and less inequality being white and being AMAB.

What unique forms of external minority oppression and stress do I experience?

Cisgenderism, heterosexism, transphobia, ableism, homo/biphobia.

Do I experience lots of psychological distress and mental health difficulties related to my intersectional identities?

Yes, I am often confronted with people who assume things about me, and expect me to be a certain kind of person. I often feel confused and like I do not belong in many places, which makes me feel awful.

Do I find it hard to move freely and easily about in the world, due to structural and institutional inequalities in the systems around me?

Yes, I feel as if I always have to hide some aspect of myself — when I am with straight people I might hide that I am gay, especially if it was in my job.

Do I feel frustrated at institutions and services for not understanding all the aspects of myself at the same time, for example health, education, social services?

When I have appointments with my GP, they often ignore everything about me, apart from my diagnosis of autism!

6 **Knowing what I now know, what do I want in my life? What needs to change? How can I look after my wellbeing better?**

I think I could be clear with people I meet that I am someone who has quite a few different aspects to myself, like we all do — I am not just Gwi with Asperger's.

I realize that in some situations, it is effective for me to 'turn down' aspects of myself, if it means I can be safe.

I realize that I can ask people for help that is specific to an aspect of my identity — this could be friends, family or my GP.

(Developed by Dr Brendan J Dunlop & Dr James Lea (2021), copyright and all rights reserved.)

ACTIVITY

THE INTERSECTIONAL PERSON: CREATING AN 'INTERSECTIONAL ME' BLANK WORKSHEET

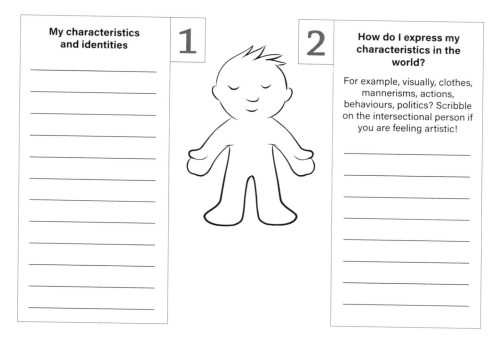

My characteristics and identities

1

2

How do I express my characteristics in the world?

For example, visually, clothes, mannerisms, actions, behaviours, politics? Scribble on the intersectional person if you are feeling artistic!

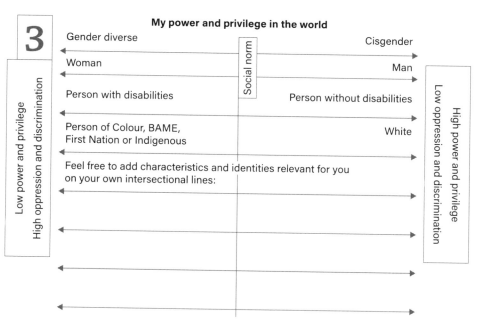

3

My power and privilege in the world

Gender diverse — Cisgender

Woman — Man

Social norm

Person with disabilities — Person without disabilities

Person of Colour, BAME, First Nation or Indigenous — White

Feel free to add characteristics and identities relevant for you on your own intersectional lines:

Low power and privilege / High oppression and discrimination

High power and privilege / Low oppression and discrimination

4 Imagine a volume button that you can turn up or turn down. In what places, and with whom, do I 'turn the volume up' on aspects of my identity?

For example, do I allow myself to inhabit my Queer identity more when I am with other Queer people?

_____

_____

_____

In what places, and with whom, do I 'turn the volume down' on aspects of my identity?

For example, do I feel less able to inhabit my British Pakistani or African American identity when I am with white people?

_____

_____

_____

In what places, and with whom, can I just leave 'leave the volume button wherever it is' and feel most comfortable being my intersectional self?

_____

5 Questions that might take more time to think about:

How do I feel in my day-to-day life?

_____

_____

_____

What power and inequality do I experience in the world as a result of my intersectional identity?

_____

_____

_____

What unique forms of external minority oppression and stress do I experience?

_____

Do I experience lots of psychological distress and mental health difficulties related to my intersectional identities?

_____

_____

_____

Do I find it hard to move freely and easily about in the world, due to structural and institutional inequalities in the systems around me?

_____

_____

Do I feel frustrated at institutions and services for not understanding all the aspects of myself at the same time, for example health, education, social services?

_____

_____

6 **Knowing what I now know, what do I want in my life? What needs to change? How can I look after my wellbeing better?**

_____

_____

_____

_____

_____

_____

(Developed by Dr Brendan J Dunlop & Dr James Lea (2021), copyright and all rights reserved.)

FINDING MY PEOPLE

How did it feel to complete the intersectional person exercise above? I hope that it did not feel too hard to try and make friends with your intersectional self. If it was uncomfortable at times, I hope that this came with some learning about yourself, and ways that you might want to tweak yourself (for you of, course), your life and/or the world at large. Generally, there are two really important realizations that we all have after doing a self-reflective exercise like this:

- We become aware of the need to find our people, our tribe, our community as a way to feel more 'ourselves' and take care of ourselves and our wellbeing!

- We realize that we can have an influence on the world around us, which can have hugely beneficial effects on our sense of who we are, our wellbeing and connection to others.

A really good way to find your people is using your friend Google (other search engines are available!). It is important to search for the intersecting aspects of your identity that you feel are most relevant, at this time in your life. For example, Queer and D/deaf; or lesbian and parent; or bisexual, British Indian and Buddhist. Remember, what you are seeking may change in the future when you want to find new tribes of intersectional people – and that is absolutely OK! Using Google, see what is around you locally. Organizations, charities, Facebook groups, 'meet-up' groups, community groups, support groups, music groups...you get the idea.

If you cannot find any relevant groups or people, why not have a really great positive influence on the world and set up a group? Many people do this using various social media platforms. You may start this group in a virtual space, but in time it could lead to in-person meets, friendships and relationships. Remember, there are people out there in the world who hold intersectional identities and want to connect with others who share some sameness to gain a sense of belonging and community.

SKILLS FROM OTHER SECTIONS THAT MAY BE USEFUL FOR YOU

- Exercises from Chapter 4, *Identity*

- Skills from Chapter 5, *Self-Acceptance and Self-Compassion*

- Skills from Chapter 8, *Feeling Anxious*
- Skills from Chapter 9, *Feeling Low*

SUMMARY

- Queer people with intersectional identities can experience unique forms of external minority oppression and stress, which can create significant psychological distress and mental health difficulties.

- Queer people with intersectional identities can find that it is hard to move about freely and easily in the world, due to structural and institutional inequalities.

- People with intersectional identities can often find it hard to be understood as the unique and glorious people they are.

- Queer people who have an understanding of their intersectional identities and have created their own 'intersectional me' can have more awareness about how they navigate the world.

- It can also help to know when and how to find our own tribe, and to know when it is helpful to challenge the world in the service of your own psychological wellbeing and mental health.

Space for your own thoughts, reflections, ideas, action plans

PART 2

SPECIFIC MENTAL HEALTH DIFFICULTIES

— Chapter 8 —

FEELING ANXIOUS

WHY WE FEEL ANXIOUS: THE FIGHT OR FLIGHT RESPONSE

Humans have evolved from other animals over thousands and thousands of years, and so have our brains. There are three 'parts' to our brains: the reptilian brain, the mammalian brain (the 'older' brain) and the human brain (relatively speaking, the newest part of our brain). Now, this is not literal. If you opened up our heads you would not see three different distinct brains. Rather, systems and parts of our brain have developed from the 'older' brains and our newer modern brain has been built on the foundations left behind by these older parts. The diagram below should hopefully make this clearer.

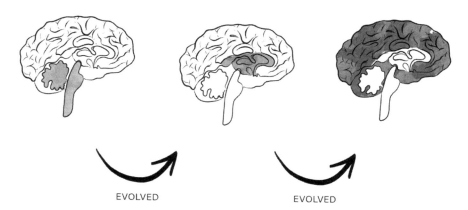

EVOLVED   EVOLVED

Figure 8.1: The evolving human brain: from survival to anxiety

Many thousands of years ago, when humans did not live in houses with phones and computers, we lived among wild animals. When we came face to face with an animal (or a human from a different tribe!) that wanted to kill us, our bodies needed to be prepared. Our old brain had a system within it that prepared us for this very situation. This system is called the *'fight or flight'* response (well, actually, the 'fight, flight, freeze, submit' response, but fight or flight is what it is most commonly known as). When fight or flight was activated in response to an external threat, our bodies literally got ready to run away from the threat, or attack it. Our hearts beat faster to pump blood to major organs, our breath became shallower to get more oxygen to our lungs, our vision narrowed to focus in on the threat and our mouths became dry (after all, who needs to eat and digest if you are about to be attacked by a huge animal?!). This physiological response meant that humans could stay alive by either running away to safety, or fighting off the threat. Very useful back in the old days, huh?

Then, more evolution happened. The human brain evolved to become bigger, and the part of the brain that is right at the front (the prefrontal cortex) developed. This is what some think of as the 'new brain'. With the new brain came fantastic new skills, such as problem-solving, the ability to focus or divide attention, planning and impulse control. Other parts of our brains, such as the area responsible for the fight or flight response, remained.

Now, here is where things get tricky. Humans do not live in the wild anymore, and rarely come up against animals that want to kill us. So, that part of our old brain that kept us safe is not really needed as much anymore. But *it is still there*. And what is more, because our brains have evolved to be able to think, plan and imagine, sometimes *just our thoughts* set the fight or flight response off.

Let us take an example. Let us say that you are a transwoman. You are walking down the street and notice someone looking at you for a few seconds. There could be many reasons why someone may look at another person out of

DID YOU KNOW?

The 'fight or flight' response evolved in humans as a survival response to external threat; namely animals that could kill us, or people from other tribes who might have tried to kill us. In the modern world, the fight or flight response can still be incredibly helpful, though sometimes it can 'misperceive' threat.

Impact on mental health

Especially relevant for Queer people, we may have grown up with adverse childhood experiences such as bullying, abuse or neglect. Our fight or flight response is likely to have kicked in in these scenarios in an attempt to keep us safe in the face of these threats.

Because humans now have the ability to replay things over and over again in our minds (sometimes called 'ruminating'), our fight or flight response can sometimes misperceive these thoughts as a sign that we are in *actual* danger again, with an immediate threat to our life. Bodily responses kick in, and when this happens frequently and repeatedly, we have come to name this as *anxiety*.

the house, but you think that this person was staring because you are trans. You may think to yourself: 'What if they are thinking bad things about me?'... and suddenly, you notice that your heart has started to beat quite fast and you are feeling your breathing get faster. Guess what? Your fight or flight response has kicked in. Your old brain thinks that your life is in danger, when actually a thought has tricked your brain into setting this system off. Now, this is not to say that your old brain always gets it wrong. It has good intent. After all, it had (and has) only one aim – to keep you safe.

If we trace this back, in this scenario there could be good reason you thought someone was thinking bad things about you. There are stories, systems, structures and policies that exist to keep Queer people, and in particular trans people, oppressed. Trans kids, like others within the Queer community, grow up thinking they are flawed, because the world they live in tells them so. Therefore, of course, it is natural to second guess other people's intentions. But there could also be so many other reasons why that person's eyes lingered for a second longer than felt comfortable to you. Perhaps they thought you were someone they knew? Or perhaps they found you attractive? Or maybe they themselves were trans and the sight of another person living life as their true self was too good an opportunity to miss seeing. While there may be good reason to be on guard, our thoughts can very quickly set off our fight or flight system. Recognizing that our thoughts have significance and can influence the sensations we get in our body (if our fight or flight response has been activated!), and the emotions we feel, is an important idea that I will come back to at numerous points throughout this book.

NOTICING WHEN ANXIETY CREEPS IN

It is a completely normal thing to experience a wide range of human emotions. Feeling jealous, happy, sad, worried, scared, excited, envious, disgusted, surprised – to name but a few! – is totally OK. Sometimes though, people can find themselves feeling stuck in one or more of these mood states and this can have unhelpful and unwanted effects on their daily lives.

Research has found that Queer people are more likely to experience low mood and anxiety when compared to cishet people (King et al., 2008; Valentine & Shipherd, 2018). Because we live in a world that emphasizes and places value on heteronormativity and binary gender roles, our fight or flight response may become activated when we feel threatened by others. This could be when faced with verbal or physical abuse, feeling disconnected or different to others, or even when we hear our own inner critical voice telling us that something about us is 'wrong'. This can lead to feelings and thoughts of anxiety.

ACTIVITY

What anxiety may feel like in your body

Tense muscles
Increased heart rate
Increased sweating
Butterflies in your stomach
Tightness in your chest
Wobbly legs
Blurred/narrow vision
Light-headedness/dizziness

What it feels like for me

_____

_____

_____

_____

_____

When these mood states (such as feelings of anxiety) stick around, people can sometimes find various aspects of their lives affected. Perhaps it is difficult to wake up in the morning, or find motivation to go to school/university/work, or you find yourself avoiding certain people/places. It can be difficult to figure out why this is happening. One way you can begin to track this is by completing a mood diary (see Table 8.1 for an example diary that you can copy). You can do this by rating your mood out of 10 (1 being very anxious, 10 being very relaxed/happy) and then noticing where you are, who you are with, what time of day it is, what has happened/is happening and so on. You could fill this diary out anytime you notice any of the physiological signs of anxiety in your body (see above), or you could routinely monitor your mood every so often (e.g., at 9am, 12 midday, 3pm, 6pm and 9pm). It may also be useful to note if you think your mood at the time is related to your identity of being Queer. It might not, but if you think it is, it can be helpful to identify how your mood is related to this.

Once you have filled this out for several days, you may be able to notice some patterns. You may notice that you always feel anxious at a certain time of the day, in a particular environment. Noticing whether this may be related to you being Queer is helpful because things in your environment could be changed to make you feel more comfortable. As we work on identifying patterns with our moods, and taking action to improve this, it is worth saying that things often start off rocky, or it can feel as if things are not getting better. As with lots of activities in this book, I would recommend sticking with them for a little while as things do and can get better.

From the example given in Table 8.1, it is clear that this person feels anxious at work when they need to use the toilet. For them, this is related to being trans, as this person does not want to be seen using the men's bathroom yet. This individual may not have needed a mood diary to make the link between feeling anxious when needing to pee and being trans in the workplace, but I hope with the example you can see how patterns related to being Queer may be identified. If the individual feels able to, they could approach their HR manager or workplace supervisor and request that some toilets be designated as gender neutral, or that sanitary products be placed in both the men's and women's bathrooms. Some companies may not have considered doing this before, and if this change were made, this person may feel less anxious at work. On page 117 is a blank mood diary. If you experience some feelings of anxiety, why not have a go at tracking your mood for a day, and noticing what is going on before you feel this way? If you are able to, I would recommend copying out the blank mood diary, because it is good to track your mood over several days/weeks to get a clear picture. There are also more blank copies available to download from https://library.jkp.com/ redeem using the voucher code EKQRFKJ.

Table 8.1: Example mood diary for someone feeling anxious

Mood I want to track: Feeling anxious

Rate your mood out of 10	Time of day	What can I feel in my body?	What thoughts do I notice in my head?	What has just happened/is happening right now?	Where am I?	Who am I with? Am I alone?	Related to being Queer?	If related to being Queer, in what way?
3	12.30pm – lunchtime	Heart beating fast Feel sweaty	'Everyone is looking at me'	I really need to use the toilet	In the open plan office	Alone at my desk, but there are lots of people sitting all around me	Yes!	I want to use the men's bathroom, but not everyone knows that I am trans
4	3pm	Heart beating fast again Bladder really hurting!	'Everyone will know I am trans if I use the men's bathroom'	I still really need the loo	In the office	Same as above	Yes	As above
7	6pm	Relief, heart rate slowed down and no longer sweating	'I feel safe now'	I have just got back home and used the loo	At home	Alone	Yes	I can pee in my own house, so others do not have to see me choose a bathroom

Blank mood diary

Mood I want to track:

Rate your mood out of 10	Time of day	What can I feel in my body?	What thoughts do I notice in my head?	What has just happened/is happening right now?	Where am I?	Who am I with? Am I alone?	Related to being Queer?	If related to being Queer, in what way?

HOT CROSS BUN AND CIRCLES OF INFLUENCE FOR ANXIETY

So far, we have covered the fight or flight response, what anxiety may feel like in your body and how to track this. Remember the hot cross bun and circles of influence from Chapter 3, *Queer Mental Health: The Basics*? It is a good idea to pull together some of the thoughts and feelings you have identified into a hot cross bun inside contextual circles. You can use the same thoughts that you already identified above. Or, now that you have had a go at doing this already, you can do this exercise with a different thought. Remember to include some of the external things that may be related to your anxious feelings (people or groups, institutions, laws and policies, or social stories). Draw arrows between some of the external things and your thoughts, feelings and behaviours if you think they are connected.

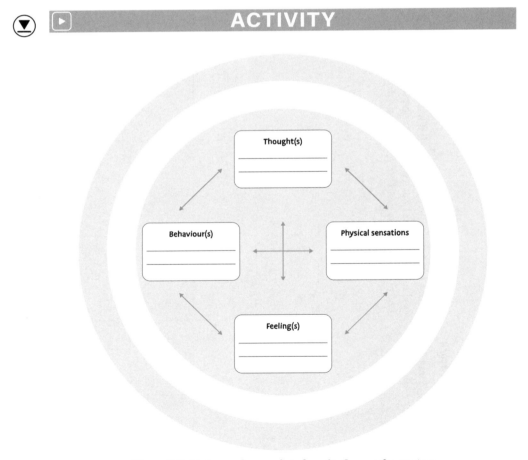

Figure 8.2: Hot cross bun and circles of influence for anxiety

WORRY

Some people can feel overwhelmed by their thoughts, and sometimes even feel as if they are going to go 'crazy' if these thoughts do not stop. This is called ruminating, or worrying, and it happens to lots and lots of people. Remember that our newer human brain is built on top of our older animal brain. Worrying is when our thoughts become sources of threat for the fight or flight response. The fight or flight response literally thinks that a thought that we are having is a source of danger! Yep, that is right, there is literally no danger outside your body, but the fight or flight response still kicks in. In fact, it does not just kick in, it goes into overdrive. This is why people can begin to have lots of thoughts in their head, and then start to feel some of the feelings of anxiety that we discussed earlier on such as feeling sick, hearts beating really fast, or a dry mouth. Because of this, the fight or flight response thinks, 'Well here we go, I *told you* something was wrong', when really it has got itself all confused. We can then sometimes believe that our thoughts were right all along, when actually we have just got caught in an unhelpful cycle (see below). Luckily, when we can recognize that this has happened, and more importantly know why it has happened, we can do something about it.

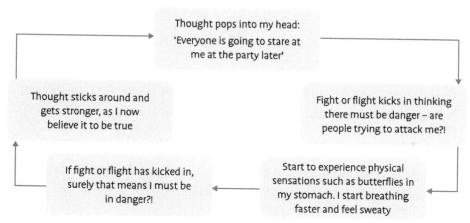

Figure 8.3: When fight or flight thinks we are in danger, and worry takes hold

DOING SOMETHING ABOUT ANXIETY: CATCHING, CHECKING AND CHANGING THOUGHTS

Something you can do when anxiety creeps in is to challenge the thoughts you may be having. Is this thought actually true, or has my fight or flight response been activated by mistake? You can do this by remembering to catch anxious thoughts when they creep in, check out how accurate or helpful they are in the situation you are in and then change them to something more helpful. Let us go through how to do this.

Catching thoughts

To catch a thought, you may have noticed a physical sensation or feeling creep in first. You may have started to think about this thought quite a lot. Or, you may be entering a situation that you know is going to bring an anxious thought creeping in (maybe a situation you have identified from your mood diary). Knowing that this is anxiety creeping in is the first step to being able to do something about this thought!

Checking thoughts

We know that the fight or flight response is around to keep us safe. However, we also know that fight or flight sometimes gets it wrong. Because of this, it is worth us checking this thought out to see if it requires us to do something. You can do this by asking yourself the following:

- Am I in danger right now?

- Am I maybe blowing the situation I am in out of proportion?

- Has my thinking become restricted to 'this' or 'that', rather than considering other options?

- Is the thought I am having telling me about the worst possible situation, rather than the most likely situation?

- Am I filtering out the good things and just focusing on the bad?

- Am I 'mentally time travelling'? Am I thinking about something that could happen, without any evidence that it will?

Changing thoughts

Once you have checked out how helpful your thought is, you can see if it needs to be changed. By answering the questions in the 'checking thoughts' section you can come up with ways to change the thought into something more helpful. For example:

- Can I assure myself I am not in danger?

- What is the most likely scenario?

- What things am I not considering, that could be relevant here?

Another good way to change your thoughts is to think of them as emails that your fight or flight response has sent to you. It may sound a little strange, but you can literally say to yourself, 'Thanks fight or flight for sending me that email, but it is not relevant, so I am going to delete it.' Imagine yourself clicking the trash can icon on your emails when you do this – it can be really freeing!

Table 8.2: Example of how to catch, check and change unhelpful thoughts

Catch it	Check it	Change it
Fingers feel tingly, get butterflies in my stomach, I start to think, 'What if I spill my drink when walking back to my table?'	I have carried hundreds of drinks back to my table before and only spilled them a few times, I will be fine I am thinking of the worst possible situation here – even if I spilled it, it is not the end of the world	Thanks fight or flight for trying to keep me safe, but spilling a drink is not going to put my life in danger Even if I did spill it, my mates and I would just have a laugh about it – it does not mean they hate me if I spill a drink!

ACTIVITY

Blank catch it, check it, change it table

Catch it	Check it	Change it

DOING SOMETHING ABOUT ANXIETY: RESETTING FIGHT OR FLIGHT

When fight or flight has been activated, but there is no real threat to manage right away, we need to have some tools to reset the physiological effects of this system, as well as the thoughts that it generates. Here are a few techniques that may be useful for you to come back to when you need them.

 ACTIVITY

Managing your breathing

It is important that we control our breathing by exhaling more than we inhale. When we take lots of short, sharp breaths, a panic attack can sometimes follow. To do this, *breathe in for five seconds, hold for five seconds* and *breathe out for nine seconds.* If this is tricky, then you can adjust the timings (e.g., breathe in for three seconds, hold for three seconds, breathe out for six seconds). This helps to bring your heart rate down so it does not feel as if your heart is going to jump out of your chest!

 ACTIVITY

Untensing your muscles

Your muscles may have become tense in preparation for fighting the threat. And what is more, you may not have realized they have tensed up! Because this exercise is about focusing on parts of your body, for some people who struggle with body dysmorphia (worrying about the appearance of different parts of your body) or gender dysphoria, you may find it more beneficial to skip this and try one of the other exercises.

We can untense any muscles by using a technique called *progressive muscle relaxation.* Starting at your toes, clench your toes together and hold for three seconds. Do the same with your foot, and then work your way up your body doing the same clench and release technique, making sure to remain clenched for three seconds. Next, move to your calves, up to your thighs, stomach, hands, arms, shoulders, neck, mouth and eyes. Notice the feeling of release when you unclench after three seconds. When you are done, scan your body – are there any other parts of your body that still feel a little tense? If so, repeat for those muscle groups/parts of your body.

Readjusting your posture

To escape a threat, our fight or flight response may have tried to protect us by reducing our size, as if to make us 'smaller' so we can hide behind something if needed. Or our hands might have become closer to our face, as if to hide us. If we remain in this small, hunched over, 'hidden' posture, our older brain may think the threat is still around. In order to help reset, it can be useful to stand up (if you have been sitting down), stretch your arms up above your head and down to your side (almost as if you are a bird trying to fly!), and lift your head high (if you notice that you are looking down). This helps us tell the old brain we are safe now.

DOING SOMETHING ABOUT ANXIETY: SAFE PLACE IMAGERY

Another way of reassuring ourselves that we are safe and resetting the fight or flight response is by visualizing a safe place in our minds. People I have worked with like to visualize walking through a forest, or walking on a beach as their chosen 'safe places', though a safe place can literally be anywhere you feel safe. Safe place imagery can work best when someone else reads out a script for you to listen to, so you can fully imagine your safe place and allow your body to relax. However, this can also work by reading this yourself. Once you have read it enough times, you may be able to remember it and be able to close your eyes and walk yourself through your safe place scene.

Below are two examples: a forest and a beach. There is also space for you to create your own safe place image, if you have a place in mind.

The forest

Find somewhere comfortable to sit, or lie down. Take a deep breath in for three seconds, hold for five seconds, and breathe out for five seconds. Once you have read this example, you might be able to close your eyes and do this yourself in your own mind.

Imagine that you are at the opening to a small, deep green forest. You notice and feel a warm summer breeze dance past your face, and the sun, although it is setting behind you, still feels warm and comforting.

Take a few steps into the forest. Notice the change in temperature – everything feels cooler under the roof of the trees. Listen to the crunch of the leaves and sticks underneath your feet. You can smell the forest air – a mix of leaves and cut grass from the nearby field.

As you walk through the forest, put your hand out and brush past the ferns and bushes. They feel both soft and crisp, warm and inviting. Perhaps you stop for a moment and feel part of the fern between your fingers.

Turning around to continue your stroll, you notice the singing of the birds. Tune into this and listen to the birds talking to each other. The sun still feels warm on the back of your neck, and the warm breeze dances past you every now and then, feeling different from the usual coolness of the forest.

Walking further along the path, you notice a rabbit in the distance. Its fur looks soft, and its nose flicks from side to side, smelling the summer air.

The sun is now low enough to scatter through the trees. As you walk along the path, notice when you walk into one of the numerous rays of light, feeling a warm spot on your face, arm or leg.

You find a log from a fallen tree and sit down to rest for a minute. While you sit here, notice the sights around you, the smells, the feelings of the sun and breeze. Sit here as long as you like, and as long as you need to.

When you are ready, stand up and walk along the path towards the other side of this small forest. You see the opening in front of you, and notice the expanse of the field on the other side. When you want to, walk through this opening and back into the field, breathing in a sense of stillness and breathing out a sense of calm.

When you feel able to, and when you want to, open your eyes. Take a deep breath in for three seconds, hold for five seconds, and breathe out for five seconds. Notice the floor beneath your feet, or your bottom on the bed or seat. Hold on to something around you to ground yourself back in this reality. And remember that whenever you need to retreat to a safe and calm place, you can come back to this forest in your mind at any time.

ACTIVITY

The beach

Find somewhere comfortable to sit, or lie down. Take a deep breath in for three seconds, hold for five seconds, and breathe out for five seconds. Once you have read this example, you might be able to close your eyes and do this yourself in your own mind.

Imagine that you are standing on an empty beach. You notice the smell of the sweet and salty sea air and can feel the sun on your face. Underneath your feet the sand is hot, though when you sink your toes in deeper you feel the cooler sand underneath.

Take a few steps forward. You can hear the sound of the waves lapping up on the shore and looking out into the ocean you notice a few boats in the distance. Apart from these boats, you are the only person around.

You take a few more steps towards the sea and notice that the sand beneath your feet has become more solid, and you are aware of the feeling of water. A wave is gently running towards you and a sudden feeling of cool wraps around your ankles as the wave hits you.

As this wave retreats, a gentle breeze passes by and your ankles feel cold as the breeze brushes past. You can still feel the warmth of the sun on your face. Notice the difference in temperature between your face and your feet.

Turning around, you walk back up the beach, away from the water. The smell of the sea is still strong and the sun is still warm and comforting.

Take a seat in the sand. Notice the feeling of warmth from the sand as you sit down. Place your hands into the sand and notice how the grains feel between your fingers. You feel calm, relaxed and safe. Sit here and notice the sounds, sights, smells and sensations for as long as you want.

When you feel able to, and when you want to, open your eyes. Take a deep breath in for three seconds, hold for five seconds, and breathe out for five seconds. Notice the floor beneath your feet, or your bottom on the bed or seat. Hold on to something around you to ground yourself back in this reality. And remember that whenever you need to retreat to a safe and calm place, you can come back to this beach in your mind at any time.

CREATE YOUR OWN SAFE PLACE

It is usually helpful to start with a breathing exercise. As you can see from the above examples, incorporating the senses can be a great way to help bring your safe place to life. To help generate your own safe place, perhaps you could begin by thinking about a particularly fond memory you have, or a beautiful or calm place you have visited. Imagine yourself in that memory or at that place and walk around this in your mind. Notice what you can see, hear, smell or touch, and write this down. If you cannot exactly remember, this is where you can get creative! Create the scene as you might have wished it to be, with whatever sights, smells and sounds you might have wanted to help you feel calm.

ACTIVITY ▶

My safe place:

DOING SOMETHING ABOUT ANXIETY: OBSERVING THOUGHTS BUT NOT ENGAGING WITH THEM

Sometimes we think that we need to do something about thoughts that enter our head. There is a specific practice (that has roots in Buddhist philosophy) called mindfulness that can be very useful in helping us just to observe thoughts, rather than engage with them.

One way of doing this is to think of the thoughts in your head as leaves on a gentle stream. Just like leaves on a stream float down the stream and out of sight, we can do this with our thoughts. Give this a go if you like. When you have finished reading this, close your eyes and when a thought pops into your head, imagine yourself next to a stream. Imagine holding your thought and placing it on a leaf that is floating towards you, before pushing it away downstream.

Another way to observe your thoughts without engaging with them is by imagining sitting in a cinema and seeing your thoughts projected on the big screen. There they are – you can see them right in front of you! But just like you would not get up out of your seat and run towards the big screen, there is also no need to do anything with your thoughts. You can just sit there, eating your popcorn (or sweets that you smuggled in because they are infinitely cheaper), and watch (or be aware of) your thoughts projected in front of you.

A final way to think about observing your thoughts is the email analogy I mentioned in the catch it, check it, change it section. Imagine that your thoughts are like emails being sent by fight or flight. When they pop into your head, you can open them, read them and then delete them, or you could just delete them straight away.

DOING SOMETHING ABOUT ANXIETY: POSTPONING WORRY FOR LATER

For someone who has been worrying for a long time, it is not easy to 'just stop'. If it were this easy, I am sure that you would have 'just stopped' by now. One way to have a better relationship with worry thoughts when they creep in is to set aside some time in the day to think about them. Lots of people tell me that worry thoughts seem to be there all the time and when they engage with them they can get stuck in a cycle, and not know how to get out. By setting aside some time in your day to engage with these thoughts, you can retain some control by saying to yourself: 'Thank you fight or flight, for letting me know something might be wrong. I will think about this later between 6pm and 6.15pm and if I need to do something I will do it then.'

By doing this you can change the relationship you have with your thoughts. Instead of them feeling like these big, scary things that control you and have power over you, you can instead exert some power and control over them.

This act of regaining control over something that might feel uncontrollable can be really important. Just knowing that you can *choose* when to engage with your thoughts is enough for some people to feel a little more in control when they feel anxious. If you have never tried postponing worry for later, I would encourage you to give it a go and see how it feels. It may take some practice. If it does not work, then that is fine. Hopefully some other activities in this section might.

DOING SOMETHING ABOUT ANXIETY: CHANGING THE ENVIRONMENT

In your mood diary, I specifically asked you to think about anything that was going on around you when anxiety crept in. This is because there may be things in the environment around us that are important for keeping anxious feelings going. For Queer people, some of these things could be related to people or groups, institutions, laws and policies, or social stories. We may have control over changing some of these things, or at least removing ourselves from these situations. Below is a table with ideas for how you could do something about anxiety by thinking about the external factors around you. A blank table follows this, so you can make this applicable to your own situation if you want.

Table 8.3: Doing something about anxiety by targeting things around us

	Contributing to anxiety	Potential solution
People or groups	Family/friends making me worry about things	Tell them they are contributing to my feelings of anxiety, or distance myself from them if I can
	Work colleagues/manager being unsupportive	Speak to someone in the workplace whom I trust to see if they can support me
	Being disconnected from other people	Reach out to friends/family who are supportive
Institutions, laws or policies	My religion/belief system is making me feel bad for being Queer	Seek out people within my religion/belief system who can support Queer people, or distance myself from this if it is doing more harm than good
	Laws are discriminatory	Reach out to my local politician and ask them to raise this at a governmental level, or start a petition

cont.

	Contributing to anxiety	Potential solution
	Policies at work are unfair	Speak to human resources about ways to make such policies more inclusive
Social stories	I am made to feel weird or odd for being Queer	Reach out and connect with people who are welcoming and accommodating of Queer people, such as support groups, online communities or local LGBTQ+ groups
	People I am hanging around with have had some kind of negative experience with a Queer person before	Have an open and honest conversation that not all Queer people are the same, and just as you might have a negative experience with a straight person, it does not mean you would avoid all other straight people

ACTIVITY

Blank table for identifying things around us that may be contributing to anxiety

	Contributing to anxiety	Potential solution
People or groups		
Institutions, laws or policies		
Social stories		

FEELING ANXIOUS AT THE PROSPECT OF TELLING PEOPLE YOU ARE QUEER

We live in a heteronormative world and, because of this, Queer people have to navigate an identity that does not fit into this dominant social story. Many people therefore feel they need to announce that they are not part of this system. This is often known as 'coming out'. As Queer people, every time we start a new job or meet new people, we are confronted with the fact that a difference between us and them could exist, and is likely going to be a conversation that we might want (or need) to have.

As I mentioned in Chapter 4, *Identity*, I prefer to think of this process of 'coming out' instead as *embracing your Queer identity* and therefore *inviting others in*. This can be both an incredibly liberating and incredibly scary experience. Understandably, you may have feelings of anxiety at the thought of telling other people that you are Queer. Your fight or flight response may have kicked in, because it is trying to protect you. For those who may not have supportive people in their lives, the fight or flight response is not entirely wrong here.

As I have mentioned briefly above, a great way to reframe this experience is to think of this discussion as being a way of inviting others into your life, rather than 'coming out' to them. The reason I dislike the term coming out is because it can have unhelpful connotations of someone hiding or not being authentic, until they tell other people. Actually, what is happened is the world has automatically assumed that you are cishet, and you have to correct this harmful assumption (usually over and over again). When you reframe this experience, this may help you feel more in control.

Below are some top tips I have for managing the experience of telling people you are Queer:

1. Only tell other people about your identity when, and if, you want to.

2. It is worth thinking about who you want to tell first. Is there a particular person you want to tell that will be supportive? If you think that other people in your life (such as family/friends) may react negatively, it is good to have at least one person who can help you navigate this.

3. Before you tell anybody, I would encourage you to try and calm yourself by practising some of the exercises mentioned in this chapter.

4. If you think the person you are telling may react negatively, it is important to be prepared for this. You could say that you will continue the conversation another day if it is not feeling helpful or safe.

5. Schedule in positive or nice things for yourself for after you make that phone call, or after you meet up with that friend/family member. What you have done can be a big thing, so be kind to yourself.

6. Do not be afraid to take up space. You have the right to exist, so do not feel as if you have to run and hide once you have told others.

7. Reach out and seek support from organizations or professionals if embracing your Queer identity is going to be challenging because the environment you are in is not totally safe for you at the moment.

8. Look forward! You have begun a new chapter in your life, so you can start to think about and plan all the things you want to do with your renewed feeling of freedom.

SKILLS FROM OTHER SECTIONS THAT MAY BE USEFUL FOR YOU

- Skills from Chapter 5, *Self-Acceptance and Self-Compassion*

- Skills from Chapter 9, *Feeling Low*

- Acceptance skills from Chapter 10, *Sleep Difficulties*

- The stress bucket from Chapter 11, *Eating Difficulties*

SUMMARY

- Our thoughts, feelings and behaviours are connected, and are influenced by things around us.

- Our fight or flight response (which evolved to keep us safe) can become activated when it perceives threat – internally or externally.

- Using a mood diary can be a helpful way to track situations that elicit anxiety for you.

- There are ways we can do something about anxiety, including resetting fight or flight, checking out thoughts and engaging with factors around us that may be contributing to anxious feelings.

- Anxiety can be managed with breathing exercises, safe place imagery or by changing our relationship with the thoughts that we have (e.g., observing them rather than engaging with them).

Space for your own thoughts, reflections, ideas, action plans

— Chapter 9 —

FEELING LOW

WHY WE FEEL LOW

Feeling low in mood is another totally normal human emotional response. We can feel low in mood if we have broken up with a partner, do not get the grades we want, lose a favourite piece of jewellery or when someone close to us dies. For Queer people specifically, feeling low can be connected to the way in which we feel different, left out or 'not good enough' for the world. Usually, this feeling lasts for a short time, but sometimes people can end up feeling low almost every day. If this feeling goes on for a long time, and affects your day-to-day activities and wellbeing, this is known as depression.

As a Queer person, there can be numerous reasons why you may be feeling low. Perhaps you have just told someone that you are Queer and they did not react how you thought they might. Maybe you have been receiving nasty messages online, or at school. Perhaps constantly having to correct other people who misgender you or use your incorrect pronouns is getting too much. Or your experience of gender dysphoria or gender envy is really difficult to deal with. We know that Queer people experience low mood and anxiety more than cishet people (King *et al.*, 2008; Valentine & Shipherd, 2018). Low mood and depression can be associated with thoughts of hopelessness and wanting to end your life, so it is really important to be aware of low mood and take steps to try and improve things.

Let us go back to the hot cross bun mentioned in previous chapters, as you might be familiar this with now. We may feel low because our thoughts, the physical sensations in our body and our behaviour are influencing (and being influenced by!) our feelings of low mood. We will add in the circles of influence (which you might now know about too) a little later. Here is an example:

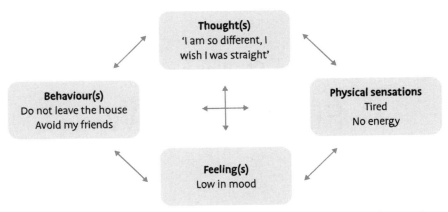

Figure 9.1: Example of low mood influenced by thoughts of wishing to be straight

When this person wishes they were straight they feel low in mood, which is understandable given the heteronormative world we live in! For this person, this seems to come with physical sensations of feeling tired and lacking in energy. When this person feels tired, they do not leave the house and they avoid their friends. Because they are staying inside and not doing much, it is likely that their energy levels and feelings of tiredness will stick around, because their body is not receiving any other input to counter this. Ultimately, this keeps them stuck in a low mood loop, because they do not hang out with their friends and have fun. Hanging out with friends is likely to signal to their body that actually this type of activity makes them feel more energetic.

ACTIVITY

What low mood may feel like in your body
Muscles feeling heavy
Fatigue/slowed down
Feeling empty inside
Feeling very tired
Headaches

What it feels like for me

_____

_____

_____

NOTICING WHEN LOW MOOD CREEPS IN

Just like for feelings of anxiety, you can track low mood using a mood diary. This helps us to see whether there are any particular situations, environments, people or activities that seem to bring on, or are accompanied by, low mood. An example mood diary is on the next page.

From this example, this person's mood seems to be consistently quite low throughout the day. They have not left their bedroom for a while, and did not get a good night's sleep. We can notice that when they felt very tired they seemed to have some unhelpful thoughts, and the same happened when they got an email from a university tutor. They also do not seem to have eaten much today, as they are quite hungry. This is perhaps influencing their decision not to go for a run – they literally have not got the energy because they have not eaten anything! It also seems that perhaps some of this person's thoughts could be connected to being Queer. For example, they are evidently a little wary of their tutor after a comment they made about them being a lesbian. When they went running last time, someone also stared at this person's rainbow socks.

By completing this mood diary this person may realize that their thoughts and feelings seem to always occur in their bedroom – I would be interested to know if they still felt as low if they were going into different rooms throughout the day, or leaving the house for a bit. There are also a few ways this person could make some small changes having tracked their mood. They could try do things to improve their sleep and try eat a little more to see if this gives them more energy to do things during the day. Furthermore, they could talk to their tutor about their identity and ask if they meant anything by their comment. Perhaps the tutor made this comment without thinking, and meant no offence at all. Equally, the person in the street staring at the rainbow socks may have been thinking how cool they looked, and meant no offence either.

On page 139 is a blank mood diary. If you experience some feelings of low mood, why not have a go at tracking your mood for a day, and noticing what is going on before you feel this way? If you are able to, I would recommend tracking your mood over several days/weeks to get a clear picture. There are more blank copies available to download from https://library.jkp.com/ redeem using the voucher code EKQRFKJ, if you need them.

Table 9.1: Example mood diary for someone feeling low in mood

Mood I want to track: Feeling low/depressed

Rate your mood out of 10	Time of day	What can I feel in my body?	What thoughts do I notice in my head?	What has just happened/is happening right now?	Where am I?	Who am I with? Am I alone?	Related to being Queer?	If related to being Queer, in what way?
2	6am	Tired	'I cannot be bothered' 'It is not worth doing anything today'	I have been awake all night – I have not been able to sleep	In my bed	Alone	Not sure	Not sure
4	9am	Heavy Body aches a bit	'Why does no one like me?'	I opened an email from my university tutor asking me why I did not submit my last essay	In my bedroom	Alone	Not sure, but he did say once, 'I did not know you were a lesbian'	Not too sure
3	3pm	Feel quite hungry Got a headache	'I should really go for a run but cannot be bothered'	Have been watching TV. Just remembered that I should go for a run	In my bedroom	Alone	Yes	Last time I went running someone stared at my rainbow socks

Blank mood diary

Mood I want to track:

Rate your mood out of 10	Time of day	What can I feel in my body?	What thoughts do I notice in my head?	What has just happened/is happening right now?	Where am I?	Who am I with? Am I alone?	Related to being Queer?	If related to being Queer, in what way?

HOT CROSS BUN AND CIRCLES OF INFLUENCE FOR LOW MOOD

So far, we have considered how thoughts, feelings, behaviours and physical sensations can be connected for low mood, what low mood may feel like in your body and how to track this using a mood diary. Remember the hot cross bun and circles of influence from Chapter 3, *Queer Mental Health: The Basics*? It is a good idea to pull together some of the thoughts and feelings you have identified into a hot cross bun inside the circles of influence. You can use the same thoughts that you already identified above. Or, now that you have had a go at doing this already, you can do this exercise with a different thought. Remember to include some of the external things that may be related to your low mood (people or groups, institutions, laws and policies, or social stories). Draw arrows between some of the external things and your thoughts, feelings and behaviours if you think they are connected.

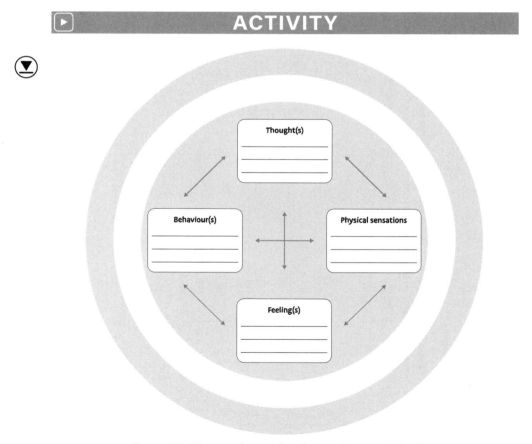

Figure 9.2: Hot cross bun and circles of influence: feeling low

DOING SOMETHING ABOUT LOW MOOD: CATCHING, CHECKING, CHANGING THOUGHTS

Just like for feelings of anxiety, we can catch unhelpful thoughts when we first become aware of them, check out how helpful these are and then change them to something more helpful or useful. Let us go through how to do this.

Catching thoughts

To catch a thought related to low mood, you may have noticed feeling quite sad, tearful, tired or demotivated first. You may have started to think about this thought quite a lot. Or, you may be entering a situation that you know may bring an unhelpful thought creeping in (maybe a situation you have identified from your mood diary). Knowing that this is low mood creeping in is the first step to being able to do something about this thought!

Checking thoughts

Sometimes thoughts pop into our head that are not helpful. Because of this, it is worth checking this thought out to see if it requires us to do something. You can do this by asking yourself the following:

- Am I maybe blowing the situation I am in out of proportion?

- Has my thinking become restricted to 'this' or 'that', rather than considering other options?

- Is the thought I am having telling me about the worst possible situation, rather than the most likely situation?

- Am I filtering out the good things and just focusing on the bad?

- Am I 'mentally time travelling'? Am I thinking about something that could happen, without any evidence that it will?

- Will this thought matter to me in a month, or in a year's time?

Changing thoughts

Once you have checked out how helpful your thought is, you can see if it needs to be changed. By answering the questions in the 'checking thoughts' section you can come up with ways to change the thought into something more helpful. For example:

- Can I bring to mind times when I did not feel worthless/like a failure and so on, to prove that my thought is not entirely true?

- What is the most likely scenario?

- What things am I not considering that could be relevant here?

Another good way to change your thoughts is to think of yourself wearing a pair of sunglasses. This is obviously making everything seem a little darker than usual. It may sound a little strange, but you can literally say to yourself, 'Right, I am going to take my sunglasses off and see if I am seeing the situation here clearly, or if things are seeming darker than they actually are.' Imagine yourself removing a big pair of silly sunglasses when you do this – it can be really freeing!

Table 9.2: Example of how to catch, check and change unhelpful thoughts

Catch it	Check it	Change it
Feel really slowed down and drained of energy	Last time I went to book club, people spoke to me quite a lot	By removing my sunglasses I can see that I am assuming the worst here
Everyone is going to think I am sucking the life out of things if I go to book club later	I am mentally time travelling here. I am assuming something is going to happen when I have no evidence for it	I have been to book club lots of times before and everyone seems to really get on with me – they always smile and invite me back, so why would they do that if I sucked the life out of things?

ACTIVITY

Blank catch it, check it, change it table

Catch it	Check it	Change it

DOING SOMETHING ABOUT LOW MOOD: SCHEDULING IN PLEASANT ACTIVITIES

Sometimes when people track their mood, they notice that there are times of the day or particular people, places or things that coincide with their low mood. When you have noticed this, you can schedule in activities to do during the day, or around these times, to improve your mood. This idea in CBT is called activity scheduling and is based on the idea of 'behavioural activation' (Veale, 2008). Basically, when we feel rubbish, we do not want to do things and this can lead us to feel even more rubbish. By acting against our awful feeling, and by scheduling in a nice activity (such as a walk in the park or a phone call with a friend), we release happy hormones in our brain and get a little feeling of having accomplished something or done something nice. By also recording these activities, and how we felt before and after, we can notice which activities 'perk' us up. Once you have identified on your mood diary the exact situations that can have an effect on your mood, you can create an activity schedule. Here is an example activity schedule based on someone's entire day:

Table 9.3: Example activity schedule

Time	Activity	How I feel before (out of 10)	How I feel after (out of 10)
7–8am	Sleep! Then wake up	–	–
8–9am	Breakfast and Instagram	5	5
9–10am	Walk in the park	5	7
10–11am	University lecture	7	4
11–12 midday	University lecture	4	4
12–1pm	Lunch! Favourite takeout sandwich	4	8
1–2pm	Go home and watch Netflix	8	7
2–3pm	Watch Netflix	7	7
3–4pm	Call friend for catch up	7	8
4–5pm	Video games	8	8
5–6pm	Dinner	8	5
6–7pm	Bath – with bath bomb	5	8
7-8pm	University work from this morning	8	4
8–9pm	Chill time – reading new book	4	7
9–10pm	Emails/bills/life admin	7	5
10–11pm	Off to sleep	5	–

By scheduling things in, you might feel a little more 'in control' of your day. Plus, you will be able to identify the activities you really enjoy, and the ones you really do not. When you are feeling low in mood, you can then schedule in more of what you know improves your mood, and avoid stuff that does not. You also do not have to do this hour by hour; it is perfectly OK just to list 'morning', 'afternoon' and 'evening' if you prefer.

From this person's activity schedule, it is clear that they do not really enjoy university work or lectures! There is the potential for them to start avoiding doing this if they know that it leads to a dip in mood. However, walking in the park, eating their favourite sandwich, video games, Netflix and calling friends tend to improve their mood. From this, it seems that when they have to do university work (boring, but has to be done!) it would be beneficial to schedule in one of these enjoyable activities afterwards, to perk them back up. Because it seems that they have a dip in mood after doing university work or attending lectures, this suggests there may be things related to this that are difficult. Maybe they could reach out to their tutors for additional support, or explore switching courses if this is the wrong course for them? Everyone's situation will, of course, be unique, but hopefully this example demonstrates that activity scheduling can identify activities that are not enjoyable and impact mood negatively (so these can be changed) as well as identify those that improve mood and can be scheduled in when you are having a rough day or know that you have to do something that may be challenging.

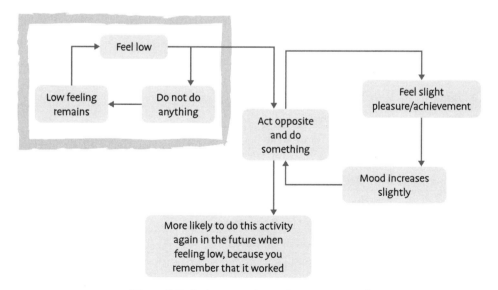

Figure 9.3: Acting opposite to change our mood

Sometimes it is difficult to think of activities to fill your day with, so here is a list of 40 things that you could try, to see if any improve your mood. By tracking what works and what does not on your activity schedule, you can do more of what makes you feel good.

1. Playing musical instruments

2. Praying

3. Going for a run

4. Listening to music

5. Watching a film

6. Planning a project

7. Sewing

8. Flower arranging

9. Painting

10. Meeting up with friends

11. Colouring

12. Gardening

13. Reading a book

14. Dressing up

15. Getting a massage

16. Picking flowers

17. Going for a picnic

18. Doing crosswords or wordsearches

19. Caring for a pet

20. Calling a friend

21. Writing

22. Going to a coffee shop

23. Doing jigsaw puzzles

24. Online shopping

25. Weightlifting

26. Recycling or 'upcycling' old things

27. Decorating a room

28. Bowling

29. Having a bath or shower

30. Repairing an old bike or machine

31. Going to the movies

32. Masturbating

33. Saving money

34. Daydreaming

35. Photography

36. Clay modelling

37. Planning a trip away

38. Writing nice things about yourself

39. Singing

40. Walking in nature

A blank activity schedule for you to fill in for yourself is on the following page.

ACTIVITY

 Blank activity schedule

Time	Activity	How I feel before (out of 10)	How I feel after (out of 10)

DOING SOMETHING ABOUT LOW MOOD: PAYING ATTENTION TO YOUR HEALTH AND WELLBEING

Our mood can be affected by lots of different things. For example, we know that our mood is linked to sleep, so if we are having difficulties sleeping then our mood may be lower. The same goes for nutrition. If we are not giving our body adequate nutrients, then this could affect our mood. By paying attention to your sleep, your nutrition (and fluid intake) and looking after your body by exercising, you are more likely to be giving your body 'happy hormones' and more likely to feel good about yourself for doing so. The same goes for exercise, however small.

If you are currently struggling with your sleep then it may be helpful to look at Chapter 10, *Sleep Difficulties*, for tips and activities for this. For nutrition and fluid intake, it might be good to add this into your activity schedule so that you have scheduled in a time to eat and drink. You can do the same for exercise by adding this to your activity schedule, even if this is going for a walk, or standing up and walking round your home!

There is probably also something to be said here about treating yourself and engaging in self-care, especially if some of the thoughts you have been having have been affecting your self-esteem. I find it quite frustrating when people tell me that they have told someone they are feeling low in mood and their only suggestion has been to 'have a nice bath'. This, by itself, is not very helpful. If only improving low mood were as simple as having a nice bath! There is something to be said, though, for doing things to treat yourself and taking care of your body, alongside some of the other activities in this section. For some this might actually be having a nice bath, or lighting some nice candles, or eating their favourite food. You could include this in your activity schedule.

However, realistic self-care can also include other things like saying no to people, making sure your voice is heard when you want it to be, persevering when you have been knocked back and knowing when something is not worth any more time or effort. I would encourage you to look back at your circles of influence and hot cross bun that you might have completed earlier on in this chapter. See if any external factors have links with how you are thinking, feeling or behaving, and whether it is in your power to change your engagement with these factors. Doing this can be a fantastic way to look after your wellbeing and take care of yourself in a positive way.

DOING SOMETHING ABOUT LOW MOOD: CELEBRATING THE SMALL STUFF

When someone is experiencing low mood, everyday tasks that other people can do without thinking can feel like huge mountains to climb. Even getting out of bed can feel like a massive thing. For this reason, it is really important to celebrate small achievements. No matter how small you think these things are, celebrate them! So, if you have managed to get up and dress yourself, when you have not been able to do this for a while, that is huge! Well done! Celebrate that. Or if you have not been able to brush your teeth for a few days and you have been able to today – well done! It is good to be able to record these achievements if you can, perhaps by writing them down on paper or on your phone. I love to-do lists, so maybe if you are able to create a to-do list of some of the small things you want to achieve on any given day, you can then tick these off, or cross them out, as you go. I know some people who hate to-do lists though, so do what is most helpful for you.

However, it is important to be quite mindful with this, and not compare your achievements on one day to the next. Just because you were able to get up, brush your hair, brush your teeth and have breakfast yesterday does not mean that it is just as easy to do that today. By making this comparison you are likely to notice self-defeating thoughts that could lead to further feelings of low mood and withdrawn behaviour. It may be good to read the self-compassion section of Chapter 5, *Self-Acceptance and Self-Compassion*, to help with this.

DOING SOMETHING ABOUT LOW MOOD: CHANGING THE ENVIRONMENT

You may have noticed from your mood diary that there are certain people, places, activities and things that accompany low mood. The same goes for your circles of influence that you might have completed alongside a low mood 'hot cross bun'. There may be quite strong links between someone or something in your life around you, and low mood. Sometimes one of the most effective ways of managing low mood is to change the environment that we are in, if possible.

I would add a caveat to this, as I do for most things in this book, of *'if possible'*. This is because I am realistic in that we cannot always change things around us. I draw your attention to this, though, in case there are things you can change. Are certain people making you feel bad about yourself? Is your job constantly making you feel worthless? Are you finding yourself drawn to people or pages on Instagram or Twitter that keep you stuck in unhelpful cycles with your thoughts? If so, it may be worth thinking about what is in your power to change this. This might be having a conversation with someone, or speaking to your boss about how things currently are for you. Perhaps you need a break from work for a little while? It may be worth disengaging from the social media people or pages that you think could be linked to your low mood and seeing if this changes things at all.

SKILLS FROM OTHER SECTIONS THAT MAY BE USEFUL FOR YOU

- Self-compassion skills from Chapter 5, *Self-Acceptance and Self-Compassion*

- Resetting fight or flight from Chapter 8, *Feeling Anxious*

- Sleep skills from Chapter 10, *Sleep Difficulties*

SUMMARY

- Low mood is a normal feeling, but when it sticks around too long it can become difficult.

- For Queer people, low mood can be caused by a wide range of factors, including feeling different and minoritized.

- Our thoughts, feelings and behaviours are connected, and are influenced by lots of things around us.

- Using a mood diary can help track your mood; you can catch, check and change thoughts, and scheduling in pleasant or enjoyable activities at the times when your mood usually dips can be beneficial.

- It is important to also pay attention to your wellbeing, celebrate small achievements and change things in your environment that might be connected to your low mood.

Space for your own thoughts, reflections, ideas, action plans

— Chapter 10 —

SLEEP DIFFICULTIES

Sleeping is something we all do. Sleep is when our brains can process things into our memory store – a bit like a computer uploading documents to a server – and keeps our cognitive skills refreshed and updated. Sleep also helps us rest and restore energy, aids our mood, and helps us repair and recover. Have you ever woken up feeling grouchy and slowed down? It might be because you have not had enough quality sleep to allow you to feel properly rested.

That said though, for lots of people, sleep is really tricky. This might be because someone cannot get to sleep at all; they keep waking up frequently throughout the night; they constantly wake up feeling tired or they are sleeping way too much. In particular, when someone really cannot sleep much at all they may see a doctor and be told they have 'insomnia' – a sleep disorder affecting the ability to fall, or stay, asleep. I will begin this chapter by providing a few facts about sleep, introducing the sleep cycle and outlining some of the reasons why sleep for Queer people can be tricky. I will then discuss how you can track your sleep to figure out what may be contributing to sleep difficulties, and I will outline some tips and tricks you can try to improve your sleep.

FACTS ABOUT SLEEP

There are lots of stories about sleep, and lots of information which is presented as if it is totally true. In fact, there is a huge amount of variability when it comes to sleep, so here are some facts, reflecting this range of variability.

- **Sleep problems are very common!** Around 95 per cent of people experience sleep problems at some point in their life.

- **The amount of sleep we need varies a lot!** Although on average people have between seven and nine hours of sleep, the amount people need can vary a lot. This also changes with age – as we get older, we tend to sleep less and our sleep becomes more disrupted.

- **It takes good sleepers roughly 30 minutes to get to sleep.** So even good sleepers do not really fall asleep straight away.

- **We do not necessarily need to 'make up' for lost hours of sleep.** We all lose sleep now and then (life can get in the way sometimes!) and our bodies will generally be OK and adapt. We never really make up for lost sleep, so this means we do not have to sleep longer one night to try and get this back. It is worth mentioning that we cannot go days and days without sleeping and still be functional. Even losing one night of sleep can significantly impair our ability to complete day-to-day tasks.

- **There are different types of sleep.** Amount of sleep is different to quality of sleep, so sometimes we can get the sleep we need despite spending less time asleep.

THE SLEEP CYCLE

Our bodies have a number of processes that naturally help us to sleep. We have a 'tiredness thermostat': the longer we are awake, the more our levels of tiredness will increase. We also have a day–night body clock. Our sleep is influenced by something called a *circadian rhythm*, and this is the body's internal clock. These two processes are normally automatic, which means that we would naturally go to sleep without thinking about it.

During a typical night, we go through different stages of sleep. This includes *light sleep* (making up approximately 50–60% of our night's sleep) and *deep sleep* (up to approximately 25% of our night's sleep). Deep sleep tends to occur in the first half of the night, and dramatically decreases as we get older. There is also a stage of sleep called *rapid eye movement* or *REM* sleep. This also makes up approximately 25 per cent of our night's sleep. This stage of sleep is associated with increased brain activity, because this is typically when information is being processed from your day. This is the stage of sleep where we dream. Finally, it is also quite normal to wake up during the night. Typically, these periods of *wakefulness* are relatively short and we fall back to sleep almost without noticing. Sometimes though, people find it difficult to get back to sleep when they wake during this stage. Rest assured, however, that wakefulness is a normal part of the sleep cycle.

The amount of time we spend in each stage of sleep varies from person to person, and also changes as we age. As we get older, sleep becomes more broken up: we are more likely to experience periods of wakefulness and need less deep sleep. Let us first start by thinking about the run up to sleep, and what is going on during the day and into the evening before you head to bed.

REASONS FOR SLEEP DIFFICULTIES

There are many reasons why someone may have difficulty sleeping. Some of these reasons may be applicable to lots of people, and some are perhaps more specific to being Queer.

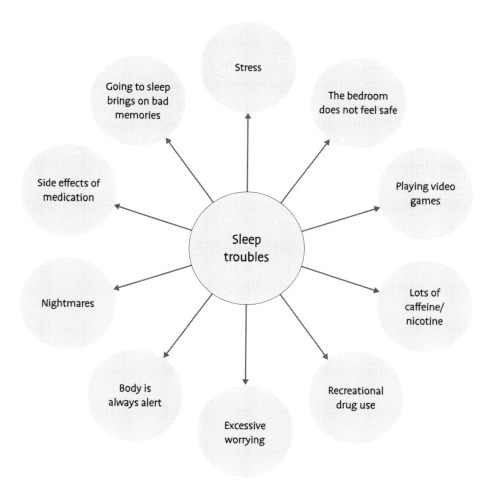

Figure 10.1: Reasons why sleep might be difficult

From Figure 10.1, you can see that some reasons for troubled sleep, such as excess caffeine/nicotine or playing video games, may be applicable to lots of people. Some reasons may be more connected to being Queer. For example, some people may report a fear of sleeping due to scary nightmares of being attacked/bullied, or the bedroom may not feel like a safe place, especially if 'going to bed' was used as a childhood punishment strategy. For some Queer people who have been sexually or physically abused, being in the bedroom or in a bed may bring on traumatic memories.

You may remember in Chapter 3, *Queer Mental Health: The Basics*, I spoke about something called 'Minority Stress Theory'. As a quick recap, this is the idea that having a inoritized gender identity or sexuality can lead to an increased experience of stress, due to stigma and discrimination. In Chapter 8, *Feeling Anxious*, I also introduced the body's threat detection system – the fight or flight response. For Queer people, experiences of minority stress may lead to hypervigilance: the fight or flight response may be constantly active and sensitive to threat. The physiological toll this can have on the body can be utterly exhausting, both physically and emotionally. Your body may be physically exhausted, so you may sleep excessively because the body needs time to recover from this constant state of alertness. Equally, you may simply be too physiologically aroused to sleep, meaning that instead you stay up all night.

It may be useful for you to have a think about any reasons you are aware of that affect your sleep. Some of the reasons listed above may be applicable to you, though everyone is unique and there might be more specific factors that stop you sleeping.

ACTIVITY

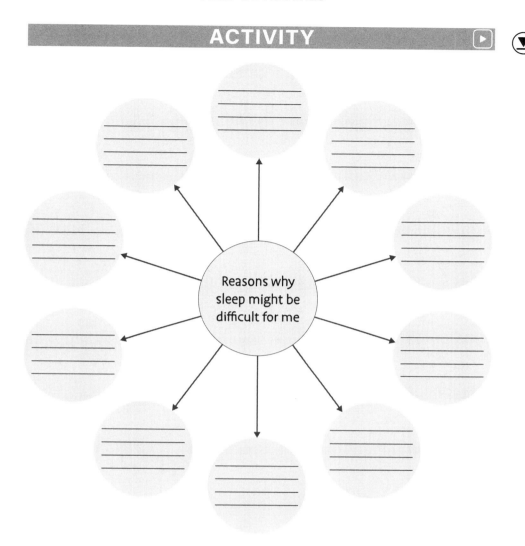

Figure 10.2: Blank sleep difficulties list

KEEPING A SLEEP DIARY

The first stage of improving sleep is recognizing how much sleep you are currently getting and what is going on before you fall asleep. Completing a sleep diary can also be a really useful tool for helping us with any misperceptions of sleep that we have, or are having. For example, some people can feel really anxious that they are not sleeping well. By completing a diary, this can show that actually someone's sleep may be a lot better than they thought, which can be reassuring. On the following page is an example sleep diary, followed by a blank copy for you to use yourself.

Table 10.1: Example sleep diary

	Monday 2 Feb	Tuesday 3 Feb	Wednesday 4 Feb	Thursday 5 Feb	Friday 6 Feb	Saturday 7 Feb	Sunday 8 Feb
What were you doing in the hours before going to sleep? Did you eat/drink/smoke?	Watching TV in my room, drank coffee	Played video games		Watched TV downstairs, then in my room	Video games	Had two glasses of wine and watched a movie	
What time did you go to/get into your bed?	11pm	10.45pm		11pm-ish	11pm	10.45pm	
Do you do anything in bed other than sleep/sexual activity?	Watched TV	Watched TV		Watched TV for a bit, went on my phone	Nintendo Switch	Watched YouTube videos on my phone	
What time did you roughly fall asleep?	1am	1am		1:30am	Midnight	Midnight	
Did you wake up at all during the night? When? For how long?	Woke up twice – once at 2am, second at 4am	Woke up at 3am because I had a nightmare		Cannot remember, but think so	Two nightmares, one at 2am, the other at 4am	Once at 3.30am	
What time did you wake up the next morning?	5am	6am		5am	5.30am	6am	
How rested do you feel on a scale of 1–10? 1 = not rested at all, 5 = somewhat rested, 10 = totally rested	2/10	2/10		3/10	3/10	3/10	

From the above sleep diary, we can see that this person missed filling in their diary for two days, but was able to do so for the remaining five days. It is totally fine if you forget to fill out your sleep diary for a day or two during the week. Just give it your best shot. We can see that this diary is showing us a bit of a pattern. This person seems to consistently look at electronic screens before bed (TV, video games, their phone), and often falls asleep in the early hours of the morning. This is several hours after they actually go up to bed. They seem to wake up several times during the night (sometimes because they have had nightmares – but they only seem to have nightmares when they have been playing video games!), and then they wake up quite early too, feeling pretty rubbish.

ACTIVITY

Blank sleep diary

	Monday	Tuesday	Wednesday	Thursday	Friday	Saturday	Sunday
What were you doing in the hours before going to sleep? Did you eat/drink/smoke?							
What time did you go to/get into your bed?							
Did you do anything in bed other than sleep/sexual activity?							
What time did you roughly fall asleep?							
Did you wake up at all during the night? When? For how long?							
What time did you wake up?							
How rested do you feel on a scale of 1–10? *1 = not rested at all, 5 = somewhat rested, 10 = totally rested*							

OVERCOMING SLEEP DIFFICULTIES: NUTRITION

It will be good to look at your sleep diary and see in the first row if you have eaten, drank or smoked in the run-up to bed. This is because there are certain things that we eat and drink that can have an impact on our sleep many hours before we actually go to bed!

Certain things that we eat or ingest are stimulants, so they increase activity in our bodies, making sleep more difficult. Take coffee, for example. Coffee (and tea and energy drinks) have caffeine in them. Caffeine is a stimulant, which means it makes us alert, and it can stay in the body for between five and ten hours after you drink it! So, if you usually go to bed at 11pm and drank a coffee at 5pm, caffeine may still be in your system, making it more difficult to fall asleep. If falling asleep is difficult for you, I would recommend that you stop drinking any caffeine after midday, so that it is out of your system by the time you go to sleep. Sugar and nicotine are also stimulants and can affect our sleep, though their effects do not usually last as long as caffeine. Avoiding sugar and nicotine in the hours before bed is probably a good thing to try too.

Alcohol is something else that can affect our sleep. Unlike caffeine, sugar and nicotine, alcohol is a sedative not a stimulant. This means that it can make us drowsy. This can be a trap for people with sleep difficulties though! Some people think that because alcohol makes them drowsy, it is a good thing to use to nod off, but this can be really counterproductive. Alcohol tends to cause us to enter deep sleep more quickly. Because our body will start to break down the alcohol once we are asleep, sleep can become disrupted. This can lead to a night of poorer quality sleep. This may also have a knock-on effect the next day: we may sleep during the day because our bodies are tired, but this then means falling asleep later that evening will be tricky.

Regardless of whether a food or drink is a stimulant or sedative, generally *when* we eat can also impact on our sleep. For example, if we eat too soon before bed, or go to bed feeling a bit hungry, we may be less likely to sleep well. As with lots of things, everyone will respond differently to different substances and foods, and it is important to figure out what you can and cannot consume close to your bedtime if you want a good night's sleep.

OVERCOMING SLEEP DIFFICULTIES: ROUTINE

Routine in the run-up to bed can influence our sleep. For example, when we do more in a day, we may find it easier to go to sleep that night. Exercising or being active during the day can help with our mood and can also reinforce the body's natural sleep–wake cycle, by making sure we are active during the day and ready for sleep at night.

When important or stressful things have happened, or are coming up, our sleep might also be affected. For this reason, it is important to find a balance. Too little activity means that we are less likely to feel tired and perhaps will not need as much sleep. However, too much activity can also be detrimental to sleep. This is especially important if the activities we have been doing have caused us to feel anxious. Bedtime may be the only opportunity during the day for us to think about the day, which can lead to overthinking and worry. Having some down-time during the day can therefore be really helpful if this is the case.

Having a carefully structured bedtime routine can be a really important way to improve our sleep. It can be helpful to think about this in two stages: the 'winding-down' routine, and the 'just before bed' routine.

Winding-down routine

- In the few hours before bedtime, it can be helpful to do something that is engaging but relaxing, and importantly does not cause stress! I would recommend checking your sleep diary to see if there is anything stressful or eventful that you are doing in the run-up to bed. Things to try can include taking a bath, reading a book, meditating, watching a TV programme, listening to music or colouring. See what works for you – everyone is different.

- Plan this activity carefully, but it is important not to be too rigid with it (there is a box on the following page to help plan this).

- Do this type of activity until you are feeling sleepy. Only then move on to the 'just before bed' routine.

Just before bed routine

- These are the activities that need to be completed just before you get into bed. This might be turning lights off, getting changed, brushing teeth, and getting into bed and getting comfortable.

- Only do this when you feel tired and when sleep feels possible, in order to forge a strong sleep–bed association.

What do I mean by 'sleep–bed' association? Well, basically, our bed is normally a strong cue for sleep, and this can be helpful when trying to get to sleep. However, when we have difficulties with sleep we may have different associations with our bed and bedtime. These can include worry, stress, hearing voices, not sleeping, nightmares, lying awake, fear and so on. This means that we may have started associating the bed with these other things, and not sleep. Only going to bed when we feel tired helps us to re-associate 'bed' with 'sleep'. This can be really tricky if the association between bed and something more difficult is really strong. But it can be changed! The following suggestions can help:

- Only go to bed when feeling sleepy.

- Do not stay in bed if you have not fallen asleep, or it feels as if you are not going to fall asleep! Get up do a soothing or relaxing activity. Perhaps have a (non-caffeinated!) drink and try again when you feel tired again.

- Likewise, do the same if you wake up in the middle of the night and are struggling to get back to sleep. It might be useful to get up for a while and return to bed when you feel sleepy again.

If you want, use the box below to make a winding-down and just before bed routine:

ACTIVITY ▶

Things I will try to wind down:

_____

_____

_____

Things I will try just before bed:

_____

_____

_____

Now we have taken a look at what has been going on in the run-up to bedtime, let us turn to focus on how you can relax and rest your body and mind, so that falling asleep is easier. This is also helpful if you wake up and struggle to get back to sleep.

In Chapter 8, *Feeling Anxious*, I introduced you to a breathing exercise. This involved breathing in for five seconds, holding this for five seconds, and breathing out for nine seconds. There is another breathing exercise in Chapter 13, *Trauma*, that you can try too. Relaxed breathing exercises such as these signal to the body that we are not in danger and can move us out of fight or flight mode.

Another activity you can try is called 'body scanning'. The aim of this activity is to notice where you may be feeling tense or anxious in your body. However, it is worth saying that because this activity is about focusing on parts of your body, if you struggle with body dysmorphia (worrying about the appearance of different parts of your body) or gender dysphoria, you may prefer to skip this and try one of the other activities.

To do body scanning, start at your toes, and move into your feet, ankles, calves and thighs. Notice any tension – are you tensing any muscles without being aware that you are doing this? Move further up your body into your stomach, and chest. Does your stomach or chest feel tight? Focus now on your fingers, up into your forearms and shoulders. How do your shoulders feel? What about your neck? Finally, think about your facial muscles – is your jaw clenched? Are you grinding your teeth? What about your eyebrows and forehead muscles – are you frowning without realizing it? Whenever you come across somewhere in your body that is holding tension or anxious feelings, tense this part of your body and give it a shake (if you can!). Practise this alongside the breathing exercise above, if you want.

OVERCOMING SLEEP DIFFICULTIES: WORRY

I introduced the concept of worry in Chapter 8, *Feeling Anxious*. As you may remember (or as you may experience yourself), worry is the process of thinking about things over and over again in our minds, and this can leave us feeling trapped and anxious.

As we have discussed in Chapter 8, *Feeling Anxious*, our brains have evolved over hundreds of thousands of years, and the older brain that houses the fight or flight response is still deep in our brains. This can be triggered by external threats, but because our newer brains have the ability to think about things, sometimes our fight or flight response gets it wrong and actually mistakes one of our thoughts for an external threat. The fight or flight response does not know the difference between what a real threat in the environment might be, and a *thought* about a potential threat. Therefore, worry sometimes sets off our fight or flight response.

This is why we can feel very anxious when we worry about things, and also why it is difficult to think or concentrate on other things. It is also difficult for us to sleep when we are in this state: in the same way that we would find it difficult to sleep if we were aware that there was a tiger prowling around outside! We can also get stuck in a cycle – our worry thoughts have led to fight or flight becoming activated, so we are struggling to sleep. At this point, people can begin to worry about not sleeping! See how this keeps us stuck in a cycle? In order for us to sleep, we need to let our fight or flight response know that it is safe for us to relax.

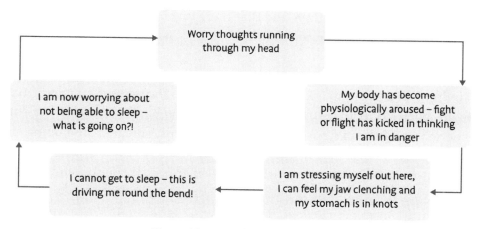

Figure 10.3: The sleep–worry cycle

So, how can we reduce our worrying? Well, there are a few different strategies that we can try out:

1. Problem-solving

There is a difference between worrying and problem-solving. When we worry, we tend not to arrive at a solution (in fact, often our worries are about things that do not have a solution). Instead, problem-solving requires clearly defining a problem, planning and taking practical action to make the situation better.

Taking a problem-solving approach can help us feel that the situation is in hand and we are moving forward. This can help reduce our worrying about it. Try to find time for problem-solving during the day. It is best to leave some space between problem-solving and bedtime. Perhaps problem-solving can be followed by a calming or enjoyable activity, like one of those listed in Chapter 9, *Feeling Low*?

2. Worry postponement

Sometimes worries cannot be solved immediately, if at all! And worrying in the meantime, especially at night, is not helpful. Worry postponement involves setting aside some 'worry time' at a particular point in the day, saying to yourself, 'I will deal with this at…' and not thinking about it until that time. Often, what we find is that when we come to our 'worry time' the worries feel much less urgent or important. That is if we can remember them at all! See Chapter 8, *Feeling Anxious*, for more information on worry postponement. As with problem-solving, make sure that your worry time is not too close to your bedtime, and that there is at least a gap between these where you fit in a calming activity.

3. Mindfulness

Mindfulness is the practice of paying attention to the present moment. This might involve noticing our thoughts, our physical bodily sensations or our experiences of the external world (sights, sounds, smells) – and doing so in a way that is non-judgemental, allowing whatever is occurring in that moment to unfold and experiencing it for what it is. It sounds simple, but can be very difficult! This is because our minds often want to wander to other things or make judgements about what is going on. However, with practice, mindfulness can be a helpful way to stop ourselves getting caught up in thoughts and worries.

A good way to begin mindfulness practice if you have never done it before is by mindfully colouring in. When you do this, pay attention to the colours, shapes and lines on the page, and notice how the pencils or pens feel between your fingers. There is a pattern on the following page that you can colour in if you like, and there are more patterns at the end of the book.

ACTIVITY

Figure 10.4: Mindful colouring: mandala

OVERCOMING SLEEP DIFFICULTIES: ACCEPTING THINGS AS THEY ARE

Accepting the fact that we are not getting sleep at a particular time can be a helpful way to reduce our worry and distress about sleep. Acceptance is a choice we make in response to these difficulties. As we have just explored, worry can have a big impact on our ability to sleep. On nights when our sleep is not going well, we can find ourselves worrying about this, which might make sleep even more difficult.

Let me demonstrate how powerful acceptance can be with a short story:

The Boy and the Donkey

A young boy had to deliver vegetables to the village. He loaded the vegetables onto his donkey and was ready to set off into town. But the donkey was not in the mood for moving. The boy became more and more frustrated with his donkey. He started to raise his voice at the donkey, and was pulling hard on the rope. The donkey dug in his hooves firmly. It seemed that the harder the boy pulled, the more the donkey resisted.

This tug of war had been going on for quite some time until the boy's grandfather arrived. He took the rope from his grandson and said, 'When he is in this mood, try this instead. Take the rope loosely in your hand, stand very close beside him and just look in the direction you want to go, then wait.'

165

The boy did as he was told, and after a few moments, the donkey started to walk.

The reason I have included this story is that we can often respond like the young boy when things are not going the way we would like them to. We often want to try harder and harder, pushing or pulling in the direction we want to go in. However, when this effort is unsuccessful, it can be more useful to follow the advice of the grandfather: to stop forcing the situation to be different and instead become more accepting of the situation as it is, for now.

It is important to realize that acceptance can be difficult. We naturally want to struggle against a situation we do not like. Therefore, acceptance can take practice. It is good to start the process of acceptance off with smaller, less important things, so that we can build ourselves up to manage accepting things that are more distressing. It can also help to break acceptance down into parts:

1. **Noticing the situation.** The first step is to become aware of the situation as it is and notice if we are engaging in a struggle with it.

2. **Allowing the situation to be as it is.** The next step is attempting to let go of the struggle and sitting with the situation as it currently is (much like the boy standing alongside the donkey rather than pulling against it). This is easier said than done! But exercises like mindfulness can be helpful here.

3. **Choosing how to respond.** Once you are fully aware of the situation and have stopped struggling against it, you then have a choice about how you want to respond. This might mean waiting for the situation to pass without wasting energy on it, or doing something differently.

Acceptance is not about dismissing our sleep difficulties, or stopping any plans we have of making changes to improve it. Acceptance can be a useful tool in the moment, when we find ourselves having a sleepless night.

Below are examples of what a sleepless night can be like when we do, or do not, choose to use acceptance. After you have read these two examples, have a think to yourself: which night would you prefer to have?

Example 1: struggling to sleep

Mario has gone to bed as usual, but finds he is unable to get to sleep. Mario begins to worry because he has an important day ahead of him and does not want to be tired for it. Mario knows that sometimes when this happens, he can lie awake all night. It gets later and later and he is unable to switch off. He starts to feel frustrated because it has been hours now and he is still not asleep... The rest of the night is spent feeling worried, upset and anxious and in the morning he feels exhausted.

Example 2: acceptance

Mario has gone to bed as usual, but finds he is unable to get to sleep. Mario begins to worry because he has an important day ahead of him and does not want to be tired for it. Mario knows that sometimes when this happens, he can lie awake all night. He notices that he is beginning to worry about it and that this is unhelpful. He decides that if he is not going to get any sleep, and if there is nothing he can do about it, it is pointless to spend the night worrying about it. Instead, he makes himself more comfortable and wonders how he can have a relaxing few hours before he has to get up (whether he falls asleep or not). He then practises some mindfulness, listens to some music and takes the opportunity to unwind.

OVERCOMING SLEEP DIFFICULTIES: CHANGING THE THINGS WE CAN

Sometimes it is also possible to consider the environment you are sleeping in, to see if anything can be changed to make things easier. You might remember the first diagram in this chapter that had different reasons why someone may be struggling with sleep. I will summarize below what you could try for some of these things.

Nightmares

Nightmares can be really scary! And they can feel super real. Some people do not like going to sleep because they are worried about having nightmares. However, nightmares are really common and loads of people get them. If you wake up from a nightmare, it can be good to first of all just ground yourself (see the grounding technique in Chapter 13, *Trauma*, for how to do this) and calm your breathing (see the breathing exercises in Chapter 8, *Feeling Anxious*). Sometimes nightmares are particularly distressing because we have woken up during, or just before, something bad was going to happen to us or someone else.

One way to get some closure when this happens is to create an ending story for your nightmare. This works particularly well for people who have strong imaginations. So, for example, imagine I had just had a nightmare that I was being chased through the street by someone. I may have woken up really scared, perhaps feeling as if someone were out to get to me. Because I never got to the ending of this situation, I may still be feeling scared now. Instead, what I could do is close my eyes and imagine myself back in that situation, but create a really funny or silly ending that makes me feel better. Maybe the person chasing me tripped up and fell down a huge ditch and rolled into a pig pen? Maybe I laughed really hard at this and then casually walked to a local ice-cream shop and bought my favourite ice-cream? Maybe I then turned into a superhero and flew off to join the Avengers?! You can make the ending of your nightmare as imaginative as you like.

It is worth mentioning that nightmares can be an experience that follows on from traumatic events. Finishing off nightmares with a funny or silly ending may help in the short term, but if you find yourself troubled by frequent nightmares, you may want to use other strategies and skills as well. I would recommend looking at the activities I present in Chapter 13, *Trauma* (in particular the self-soothe box and TIPP skill sections), which you could perhaps use alongside this, if this is relevant for you.

Medication

Some medication that you take may render sleep tricky. I would recommend speaking to your doctor if the medication you are taking is causing sleep difficulties, as your doctor may be able to switch you to something else or alter the amount you are taking. There are also some medications or supplements that your doctor can prescribe or advise to help with sleep, if you want this. I would advocate trying some of the things in this section first, and if these do not seem to be helping, then perhaps speak to your doctor about this. Medication for sleep difficulties works for some people and not for others – we are all different!

Video games/mobile phone scrolling/watching TV

As highlighted previously in the sleep diary example, playing video games before bed can physiologically arouse us, making sleep difficult. Try stopping playing video games several hours before bed, so you can engage in your wind-down routine. If you play video games in your bedroom, then try and move your games console/computer/TV out of your room so you begin to associate the bedroom just with sleep. The same goes for your phone. I am guilty of this myself as I go on my phone all the time in bed, but if you are struggling with sleep, leave this in another room. Of course, if you wake up in the night you can go and use your phone and come back to bed when you are sleepy, but try and keep it separate from your sleep space.

The bedroom does not feel safe

The bedroom may be a room that does not feel safe for some Queer people. Perhaps you were made to go to your room as a punishment. Some people may have experienced abuse or assault in the bedroom. Of course sleep is going to be difficult if the room you are sleeping in does not feel safe. My first thought is that if it is possible (and you wanted) to move your bedroom to another room in your house, then try that. If you live in a flat, studio or bedsit, perhaps try just moving your bed to another area. Sometimes physically changing the geography of our living space can help with memories or associations we have.

Next, try and make your sleeping space as comfortable as possible. Remove anything that has negative or unhelpful associations out of this area. Fill your space with things that are relaxing, safe and calming. This could be photographs, pictures, soft toys, furnishing or candles. Sometimes people say that their room is not dark enough and this can affect how safe or containing the room feels. If this is the case, try to make your room darker by getting some blackout blinds or thick curtains.

Sleep brings on bad memories

Sleep itself may trigger bad memories, especially if an individual experienced any kind of abuse or trauma in the bedroom or while they were sleeping. My first piece of advice would be to look back at your sleep diary, as mentioned above, to see if you can notice any patterns. Are there specific memories or images that seem to occur just before you go to sleep? Is there a pattern to these? This may give you an indication as to what you could try changing in the environment to make things slightly easier to manage. Some of the things I have mentioned above about making the bedroom a safe place might be helpful here, and activities within Chapter 13, *Trauma*, might be useful to try too. Activities from the *Trauma* chapter that you might wish to start with include including creating a self-soothe box and the grounding technique.

SKILLS FROM OTHER SECTIONS THAT MAY BE USEFUL FOR YOU

- Self-compassion skills from Chapter 5, *Self-Acceptance and Self-Compassion*

- Resetting fight or flight from Chapter 8, *Feeling Anxious*

- Creating a self-soothe box from Chapter 13, *Trauma*

- The grounding technique using five senses from Chapter 13, *Trauma*

SUMMARY

- Sleep is something that all humans do, although the amount of sleep we need depends on the individual.

- There can be numerous reasons why Queer people struggle with sleep, including nightmares, feeling anxious or the fact that going to sleep just is not safe where they are.

- Using a sleep diary can help us to track what is going on in the run-up to sleep, so that we can consider changing things such as what we eat or drink before bed, and what our bedtime routine is like.

- Worrying in bed can keep us awake, and things such as worry post- ponement, mindfulness and acceptance can be used to try make this easier to manage.

- Sometimes one of the most effective things to do for improving sleep is to see if there is anything in the immediate environment that we can change, such as making the bedroom feel like a safer place to be or considering side effects from medication.

Space for your own thoughts, reflections, ideas, action plans

— Chapter 11 —

EATING DIFFICULTIES

WHY PEOPLE CAN STRUGGLE WITH EATING DIFFICULTIES

Anorexia, bulimia and binge eating may be terms you have heard of. Anorexia is characterized by extreme restriction of food and fear of gaining weight. Bulimia is typically characterized by cycles of bingeing (eating lots of food at all once and it feeling out of control) and purging (expelling this food by vomiting or by using laxatives) as well as other behaviours such as food restriction, missing meals, using diet pills and excessive exercise. Finally, binge eating disorder is a label given when people experience a loss of control over their food intake, eating large amounts of food in a short period of time, and are distressed by their behaviours around food. These are diagnoses that can be given to people who experience difficulties with food, but you do not need a specific label from a professional to recognize that you have a difficult relationship with food.

Lots of people struggle with restricting their calorie or nutritional intake, or with bingeing and purging, excessive comfort eating (some people call this 'eating their feelings') or just avoiding certain foods altogether. Some people use excessive exercise as a way of managing weight, and this can become obsessive and unhealthy for the individual. Eating difficulties can be linked to a wide range of things. These include things specific to you, such as weight, body image or emotional dysregulation. Equally, things that are not specific to you may also influence your eating patterns. These can include poverty and availability of certain foods, peer pressure, and social stories about food and relationships. Experiencing trauma, stories that exist within family environments and feeling a sense of not belonging to a community or group are also linked to difficulties with food.

Some people have specific thoughts and feelings associated with their eating difficulties. Sometimes this is linked to control – someone may feel 'out of control' in other areas of their life and find that food is one of the few things they feel able to control. For others, eating difficulties are linked to feelings of safety. Perhaps regulation of food or drink provides someone with a sense of consistency and predictability that is otherwise absent. People also describe eating difficulties as being linked to emotional regulation: to 'feel something' when they are otherwise feeling numb; or to punish themselves if they are feeling shame or guilt. What is important for me to flag to you is that no matter what may be specifically linked to someone's eating difficulties, the things that people do to manage can actually end up keeping their eating difficulties going. For example, as people lose weight, they may become more consumed with thoughts about food or their body. If people restrict their food intake, then physiological responses from the body make it much more likely that bingeing will result. It is worth saying that we know there are universal effects of restricting food. The famous 'Minnesota study' by Keys and colleagues (1950) found that without regular food intake (and therefore when people do not maintain a regular body weight), social, psychological and behavioural consequences can follow. This study used methods which are widely viewed as unethical by modern standards, though the take-home point I hope to demonstrate by referencing this study is that by not giving the body what it needs, we know for sure that changes in our thinking skills, changes in bodily function and changes in our emotional wellbeing will follow. For example, some people may become overly rigid in their thinking. Or they may have difficulties shifting from one topic to another and can focus in on a very detailed view of seeing things when it comes to food and views of the self. These changes in thinking, alongside other psychological and behaviour consequences which happen because of restricted food intake, can then end up actually keeping eating difficulties going. Because of this, some people may not even be able to recall what started their eating difficulties off, or the reasons for continuing with an eating habit may have become unclear.

It is important for me to say that I am not a medical doctor, and people who experience eating difficulties should ask advice from a medical doctor as soon as they can, as well as seeking help from a mental health professional. This is because altering our food and drink intake can have consequences for our bodies that are not always visible on the outside (such as problems with digestion, hormonal changes, organ and muscle problems, issues with the heart and circulation, and bone density problems). While I can provide some general activities for you to think about in relation to any eating difficulties you may have, it is likely that you would benefit from more specific, targeted support. Such support can be implemented by a range of professionals, including mental health professionals, medical doctors and dieticians. Your general practitioner (GP) or family doctor is a good person to start these discussions with, although there are also charities (listed at the end of the book) that can point you towards local services in your area.

WHY QUEER PEOPLE CAN STRUGGLE WITH EATING DIFFICULTIES: UNREALISTIC BEAUTY STANDARDS

Evidence tells us that Queer people struggle with eating difficulties more than cishet people (Feldman & Meyer, 2007; Parker & Harriger, 2020). This is particularly the case for the incidence of anorexia and bulimia in gay and bisexual men. There are going to be some Queer-specific reasons for this, one of these being the unrealistic beauty ideal that Queer people tend to strive for. Fat-shaming within the Queer community is a particularly prevalent difficulty that goes hand-in-hand with this. Physical beauty is held in such high esteem in some parts of the Queer community, because rejection from the mainstream norm of cisgender heterosexuality forces us to amplify our desirability within the Queer world. In other words, we absolutely do not want to be rejected again. Add to this the powerful social stories about slimness and muscled bodies that generally exist, and this creates a kind of unspoken competition between Queer people – worthiness and acceptance become equated with physical attraction.

This can create very unhelpful cycles. Lots of people can internalize the idea that they are only worthy and deserving of love and acceptance if they are physically attractive. So some people start to get fitter with the aim of being more 'attractive', often by manipulating what they are eating, or doing. These people may start doing things like restricting what they are eating, doing super demanding diets or exercising more often. Or, if someone is trying to become more muscular, they may become particular with what they eat, they may 'live in the gym' and prioritize it over other things, and even use steroids or other substances to achieve a more muscular physique. This is not because they necessarily want to, but because the need to fit in is such a strong driving force for us as humans, and sadly fitting in only happens when we think we are doing what others expect of us. All of these behaviours can have significant physical and psychological impacts, and can make us feel worse about ourselves.

Figure 11.1 shows the cycles that I have discussed above. As you can see, unfortunately, no matter what is tried, people tend to end up still feeling as if they have not quite achieved what they wanted (because they were perhaps trying to achieve the impossible for their body type and/or lifestyle). And so the cycle begins again, keeping us stuck in a loop that feels really tricky to break. It should be noted that I have simplified some of the processes in the figure below to demonstrate broadly what could be going on. The thoughts, behaviours and feelings I mention within the figure are complex and will be unique to different individuals.

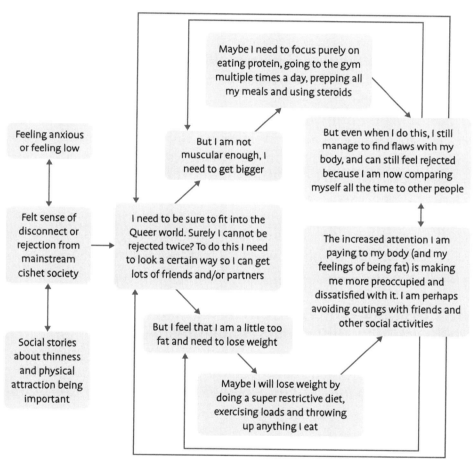

Figure 11.1: Getting stuck in unhelpful eating cycles

WHY QUEER PEOPLE CAN STRUGGLE WITH EATING DIFFICULTIES: MANAGING GENDER DYSPHORIA

Some trans and gender diverse people may feel uncomfortable with their bodies, because this may not fit with their own internal sense of self. There are natural processes that bodies go through, which can differ based on whether and how the body is producing oestrogen (a female sex hormone) or testosterone (a male sex hormone). For example, if someone's body is producing testosterone, they may begin to develop a more pronounced jaw line, broader shoulders and greater muscle mass. If these physical features (which are typically socially ascribed to men) do not fit with your internal sense of self, this can cause something called gender dysphoria. Gender dysphoria is when your physical body, or features of your body, do not fit with your internal sense of gender, and this can create psychological distress. This is equally true for people who produce oestrogen: this can lead to wider hips, increased body fat ratio and breast development. Again, if these features (typically socially ascribed to women) do not align with your sense of self, this can be incredibly distressing.

It is no wonder then that people try to do what they can to change their physical appearance! Sometimes, however, this has unintended conseoquences, and can have effects on our bodies that we just were not expecting. Some of these unintended effects can be life-altering. So, even though restricting food, excessively exercising or binge eating may seem to help with changing the physical appearance of your body temporarily, this can have serious adverse effects on internal organs, especially if it is done during adolescence or early adulthood when the body is still developing.

WHY QUEER PEOPLE CAN STRUGGLE WITH EATING DIFFICULTIES: MISOGYNISTIC SOCIAL STORIES

Especially relevant for Queer women are the body ideals connected to misogynistic images and assumptions of women's bodies. The pervasive and hugely damaging social story that women's bodies exist to serve the sexual needs and gratification of men (women's bodies are their own and are *not* under the control of other people) means that women can often struggle with their body image and weight, due to internalized misogyny. This is a form of misogynistic power, because men (or rather the patriarchal system that exists around us) are influencing and controlling women's bodies.

For Queer women, there is an added layer of difficulty here. Remember Chapter 7, *Intersectionality and Me*, in Part 1? Queer women (and people gendered by others as women, who might instead consider themselves as agender, non-binary or genderfluid) have to navigate their identity as a woman and their identity as Queer, and therefore institutions and systems of oppression attached to both identities must be confronted. It can be exhausting and traumatic for Queer women to be subject to male beauty standards. The pervasive social story that the very essence of being a woman is to please (and look pleasing) to a man, may be the furthest thing from their mind! Because of this social story that exists, lots of lesbian and bisexual women will feel the pressure to look a certain way, creating an assumption among Queer women that the 'male-approved' body standards are the norm among Queer women too.

For some, the driver for eating difficulties is not meeting a male-defined beauty standard per se, but rather, the act of being judged based on appearance, full stop. Judging women for their appearance may not be about whether they are attractive or not to the male gaze, but rather the belittling of women by saying that all they are good for is reproduction, rather than owning and embracing their own identity. As with gay and bisexual men, this can then create a dominant story and norm that looking a certain way is the only way to feel attractive or *worthy* to others. Of course, this is an ideal that many cannot keep up with or achieve. There are disproportionate levels of obesity among lesbian and bisexual women (Boehmer, Bowen & Bauer, 2007; Struber *et al.*, 2010). Given the multiple societal challenges that Queer women have to navigate, it is plausible to suggest that such emotions are managed by some people through comfort eating, though there is a complex interplay going on here with lots of other social, psychological and physical factors.

UNDERSTANDING WHY I MIGHT STRUGGLE WITH EATING

As I have introduced in Chapter 8, *Feeling Anxious*, and Chapter 9, *Feeling Low*, the first step in changing patterns of behaviour is to become more aware of them. A great way to do this is by tuning in to your eating, drinking and exercise habits, and noting down thoughts and behaviours in a journal. This can be really helpful for noticing patterns. For example, do certain thoughts tend to lead to restrictive eating? Do certain things in the environment make this behaviour more likely? Are certain bodily sensations linked to your eating patterns? Thinking about whether any particular eating difficulties are linked to aspects of your Queer identity is also helpful, and we will think about this more towards the end of the chapter. Let us go through an example together for Faisal, a gay Muslim cisgender man.

Table 11.1: Example eating difficulties journal for Faisal

Eating difficulty I want to become more aware of: bingeing and purging

Rate your mood out of 10	Time of day	What can I feel in my body?	What thoughts do I notice in my head?	What has just happened/is happening right now?	Have I eaten/drunk anything? If so, what?	Where am I?	Who am I with? Am I alone?	Related to being Queer?	If related to being Queer, in what way?
3	4pm	Hunger pangs	'I am so hungry'	I am eating all the food I can in the fridge	Left over takeaway, yoghurts, packet of cheese, tub of ice cream	At home	Alone, but just come back from visiting parents	Not sure	
2	5pm	Feel really full Feel sick	'I am disgusting' 'I am a sinner'	I was thinking about what my parents would say about me eating all that food I have just gone to the bathroom to be sick	No	At home	Same as above	Yes	My parents have said I am a sinner because being gay does not fit with their idea of Islam – I feel incredible shame
3	11pm	Quite tired and exhausted Feel anxious	'No one will ever love me'	On a dating app, someone has just said, 'You cannot be gay and Muslim' I have gone to the bathroom to be sick again	No	In my bedroom	Alone	Yes	The person on the dating app has reminded me of my identity as a gay Muslim, and has made me think about what my parents would say

Faisal is experiencing difficulties with bingeing (eating a significant amount of food all at once and a sense of loss of control around eating) and purging through vomiting. From his journal, we can see one incidence of bingeing at 4pm, followed by purging at 5pm and again at 11pm. Faisal's mood is consistently low when he does this, which gives an indication that this tends to happen when he is feeling low or anxious. Also, we know that restricting food and vomiting can lead to changes to our blood sugar (for example). When blood sugars are low this can increase the likelihood of bingeing. It appears on this occasion that Faisal did not eat until 4pm, and felt hunger pangs before eating anything he could find in the fridge. When he purged an hour later, we can see that he had some really distressing thoughts about being 'disgusting' and a 'sinner'. Faisal appeared to have been thinking about what his parents would have said about him eating all that food at once. This judgement from his parents made him think about other judgements they have about him, and he linked this to being gay: his parents have told him that being gay is a sin within their interpretation of the Qur'an. Later that evening, when Faisal received a message on a dating app saying that being gay is incompatible with being a Muslim, this again seems to have made him think about his parents and what they would say about his identity. For Faisal, it appears from this brief insight into his eating difficulties that these behaviours could be linked to managing some difficult feelings around connecting with others and feeling like a 'sinner'. This is connected to being Queer, given his intersecting identity as a gay man and a Muslim.

On the following page is a blank eating difficulties journal for you to use, if you wish. As I have mentioned before in other chapters, it is a good idea to try and notice and observe these difficulties over several days or weeks so that you can get a clear picture as to what thoughts, feelings or situations may be associated with your eating difficulties. Extra copies of this journal can be downloaded from https://library.jkp.com/redeem using the voucher code EKQRFKJ.

Blank eating difficulties journal

Eating difficulty I want to become more aware of:

Rate your mood out of 10	Time of day	What can I feel in my body?	What thoughts do I notice in my head?	What has just happened/is happening right now?	Have I eaten/drunk anything? If so, what?	Where am I?	Who am I with? Am I alone?	Related to being Queer?	If related to being Queer, in what way?

Importantly, thoughts and feelings associated with any eating difficulties you have can be very specific and individual. From your eating difficulties journal, you may have begun to see some patterns and links between certain thoughts, feelings, physical sensations and any specific eating/drinking/exercise behaviour you do. If we think back to Chapter 3, *Queer Mental Health: The Basics*, again, and the 'circles of influence' that exist around us, it is important as well to be able to situate our own personal understanding of what is going on within this broader context. For Faisal, for example, it seems pretty clear that his family, and his faith, seem to be external influences that are affecting his behaviour. There might also be wider social stories about being a Brown man, or a gay Brown man, that have influence here. Racism may also be linked to some of the thoughts and feelings that Faisal is having, which in turn could have links with his eating behaviours.

On the following page is a blank copy of a hot cross bun inside the circles of influence. If you think it would be helpful, have a go at first completing your own hot cross bun (which could be based on your eating journal, or something else) before thinking about what could be influencing this externally.

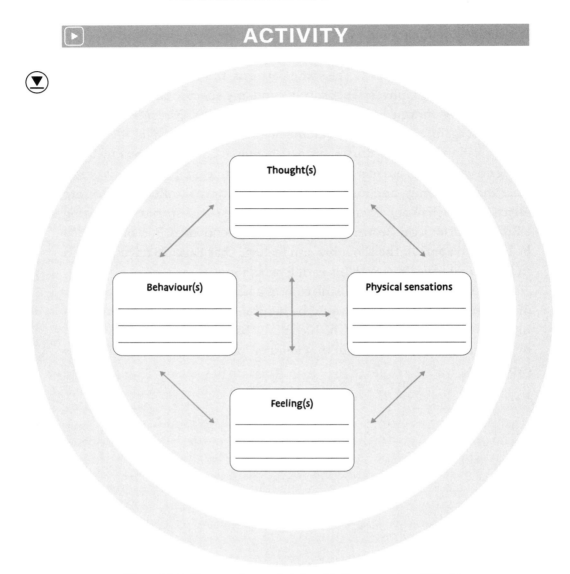

Figure 11.2: Hot cross bun and circles of influence: eating difficulties

DOING SOMETHING ABOUT EATING DIFFICULTIES: RECOGNIZING THE FAKE FRIEND

Restricting what you eat, bingeing and purging, other eating difficulties and excessive exercise can be really distressing. Other people in your life may have noticed your weight loss/gain, or the fact that your weight is going up and down a lot, and have commented on this, which can add to distress. Sometimes though, the 'fake friend' that is your eating difficulty may be convincing you that everything is OK, and that some of the stuff you are doing is totally normal or will help you get to where you want to be. For this reason, the fake friend can make people believe that what they are doing is more important than anything negative that might happen because of it. Almost as if this fake friend is saying, 'Just chill out nothing is wrong!', when actually this is a lie.

The first step in doing something about these behaviours is to recognize that this particular difficulty has crept into your life. By completing the eating difficulties journal, hot cross bun and circles of influence, you may already have started to recognize that this is something tricky in your life that needs attention. Because eating difficulties can convince us that there is nothing wrong, they have a lot of power in our lives. Thoughts that may pop into your mind, such as 'I really need to be thinner', usually belong to the eating difficulty, trying to convince us that being thin is what we should be striving for, and that there is nothing wrong with restricting food in order to achieve this. Eating difficulties can therefore be thought of as fake friends that have strolled into our life trying to be our bestie, when in actual fact they want nothing more than to see us fail.

For the purposes of this part of the chapter I am going to refer to 'eating difficulties' as 'Eddie', to demonstrate how unhelpful Eddie can be. Eddie's power comes from their ability to isolate us, and convince us that we are alone and that they are the solution to our problems. Doing this is in Eddie's favour – if we are alone and cut off from other people, then we are more likely to listen to Eddie as they appear to be our only friend. Recognizing that Eddie is doing this can help us to reduce Eddie's power, by going against what they are trying to make us do. If you notice that you seem to be spending more time alone and not engaging much with friends or family, then one way to reduce Eddie's power is to act opposite to what they are telling you to do. Spend time with friends, family and other people! If you feel comfortable, tell other trusted people about Eddie and the fact that they are in your life at the moment. Having just one other person in whom you can confide about Eddie is a way of getting help and support, and helping you to see Eddie's tricks for what they are. This is a great way to reduce Eddie's power.

Because Eddie can make people feel really isolated, it might be a good idea to list the names of several people you trust, to whom you might be able to talk about Eddie. You do not have to do this right away – it can take a lot of courage to tell people about these types of difficulties. But at least the names of people will be here when you feel able to.

ACTIVITY

A trusted friend: _____

A trusted family member:_____

A helpline I could call: _____

A trusted healthcare professional:_____

A trusted colleague at work: _____

A trusted teacher/lecturer:_____

Others I trust: _____

Others I trust: _____

Others I trust: _____

DOING SOMETHING ABOUT EATING DIFFICULTIES: SEPARATING EDDIE AND ME

Eddie can make it feel as if there are no other 'parts' to ourselves, and therefore listening to them is the most effective thing to do. Sometimes, it is good to try and attribute qualities to Eddie, so you can understand how Eddie differs from you. A good way of doing this is to describe exactly what Eddie might look like, what they sound like, what their name is (you may have a different name other than Eddie!). Then, you can do this same exercise for another part of you that is separate from Eddie. Doing this exercise can be really useful when Eddie is feeling very powerful in your life. What is more, if you have got a good imagination, perhaps you can change how Eddie looks and sounds, so that you can remind Eddie that you are the one in charge around here!

ACTIVITY

Building up a picture of Eddie

_____

_____

What does Eddie look like? (Tall/small? What clothes do they wear? Any tattoos/ piercings?)

_____

_____

What does Eddie sound like? (Tone of voice? Are they quiet/loud? Squeaky/ deep?)

_____

_____

What is their name, if not Eddie?

_____

_____

How do they behave? (Controlling/quiet? Manipulative?)

_____

_____

Building up a picture of the part of me that is separate from Eddie

_____

_____

What does the part of me separate from Eddie look like? (Tall/small? What clothes do they wear? Any tattoos/piercings?)

_____

_____

What does this part of me sound like? (Tone of voice? Are they quiet/loud? Squeaky/deep?)

_____

_____

Do I have a name for this other part of me, or is it just my name?

_____

_____

How does this part of me that is separate from Eddie behave, or how would I want this part of me to behave? (Life of the party? Funny? Academic?)

_____

_____

DOING SOMETHING ABOUT EATING DIFFICULTIES: ADDING MORE COPING STRATEGIES

Some people may notice from their eating difficulties journal, or just from general patterns that they have observed in their life, that Eddie seems to have most power when they are stressed. This links back to one of the functions of eating difficulties: they can help people feel more in control when other things feel out of control. If this is relevant for you, then a good way to manage it is to ensure that you have strategies, skills and positive things in your life to help you deal with situations that may feel stressful and potentially chaotic.

A good visual metaphor for this is the 'stress bucket'. The idea is that the bucket represents our life, or a particular point in our life. The water pouring into the bucket represents life's stressors. These may be general stressors such as arguments with other people, worries about money or stress at work. For Queer people, there may be additional stressors related to being Queer such as discrimination, exclusion, the presentation of 'thinness' as an ideal or being misgendered. When all these 'cups of water' are poured into our bucket, we can get full up very quickly, and our bucket may overflow.

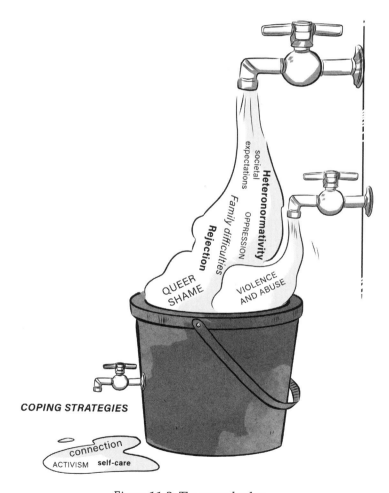

Figure 11.3: The stress bucket

So what we need to do is find a good way to keep the water levels down, so that even though stress may pour in from the top (because let us face it, life is not always rosy and there are likely to be things that come into our lives that are stressful) we can release some of this stress through the tap at the bottom of the bucket. This tap represents our coping strategies – those strategies, skills and positive things in your life that you can use to manage the stress.

Now Eddie can often work well for us, and because we know they seem to work, we are more likely to use them when faced with stress in the future. Plus, it is hard to try new things out when you are stressed. This is by no means presenting eating difficulties as just coping strategies when faced with stress, because we know that such difficulties are hugely complex, can serve multiple functions and may have very personal meanings for us. What I hope to do here though is recognize that part of an eating difficulty can be about managing stress, and that Eddie can rear their head especially in times of stress. Therefore, if you recognize that Eddie seems to become more prominent or powerful when you are stressed, then it is worth thinking about how we can ensure that there are multiple 'taps' attached to your stress bucket, so you can manage stress in other ways.

First, it might be good to recognize some stressors or things that can make you worried, anxious or stressed, in particular at times when your way of managing this may be related to food or excess exercise. You may have started to recognize or pinpoint some of these from the earlier exercises, and you can absolutely add them in here too if they are relevant. It could be helpful to think about which stressors are more 'general' stressors (I have put some examples on the left), and which might be connected to your experience as a Queer person (I have put some examples on the right). Below is a blank stress bucket for you to be able to list some of these things:

ACTIVITY

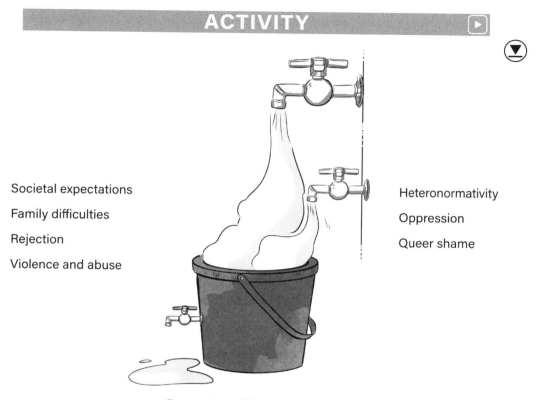

Societal expectations

Family difficulties

Rejection

Violence and abuse

Heteronormativity

Oppression

Queer shame

Figure 11.4: A blank stress bucket

At the moment, Eddie may be convincing you that restricting food, bingeing and purging or exercising a lot are good coping strategies that you can use to manage stress in your life. And I have no doubt that these strategies may have been useful for you in the absence of other things. Of course, if we find something that seems to work, and seems to make things feel more manageable, why would not we use it? So, totally no judgement here about that. What is important to recognize, though, is that as I mentioned before, Eddie can have a lot of power over us and can convince us that we do not have other coping strategies or resources, when actually, we might. We can learn new ways of managing things which do not come with the cost and consequences of eating difficulties. But Eddie would not tell us this; it is in Eddie's best interests to make us believe they are the best option. If we find other ways of coping, then maybe we will not need Eddie anymore, and Eddie wants to stick around.

So, for your stress bucket you want to be able to identify other coping strategies or resources that you have, so that you can try using these next time instead of doing what Eddie tells you might be good. There are several activities or strategies from other sections that you could try:

- TIPP skill from Chapter 13, *Trauma*. Just be aware though that this may not be the best skill for you to use if excessive exercise is part of, or linked to, your difficulty.

- Self-soothe box from Chapter 13, *Trauma*.

- Safe place imagery from Chapter 8, *Feeling Anxious*.

- Breathing exercises from Chapter 8, *Feeling Anxious*.

- Mindfulness exercises from Chapter 10, *Sleep Difficulties*.

In the following box, I have listed lots of other things that people use as coping strategies when they are very stressed. Some of these can be used as a means of simply distracting you until you feel slightly calmer. These are not necessarily 'solutions' to difficulties, but rather tools that can be used to help manage when things are getting tough. See if any of these feel relevant to you, or feel like something you could try:

Going outside for fresh air	Lighting a candle and observing the flame/smell
Painting/colouring	
Reading a book	Talking with a family member
Photography	Engaging in your favourite hobbies
Watching funny videos online	Listening to music
Playing with your pet(s)	Making a to-do list, and prioritizing stuff
Calling a friend	Popping bubble wrap
Ripping up bits of paper	Letting others know you need space
Shouting/screaming into a pillow	Yoga/meditation
Gardening	Writing in a journal/diary

It might be good to make a list of six coping strategies (or as many as you can think of) that you could try when you can feel yourself becoming stressed. You can use any of the above example strategies, or you can think of your own.

ACTIVITY

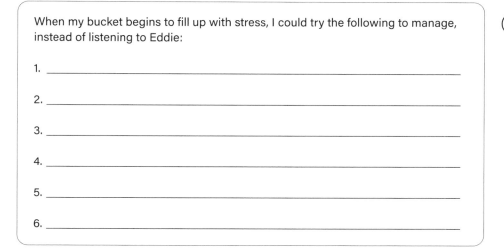

When my bucket begins to fill up with stress, I could try the following to manage, instead of listening to Eddie:

1. _____

2. _____

3. _____

4. _____

5. _____

6. _____

DOING SOMETHING ABOUT EATING DIFFICULTIES: REINTRODUCING FOOD

At first, the thought of regular or consistent eating may feel quite upsetting and difficult. With time, and using some of the skills that are provided throughout this book, this will become easier. Regular eating has numerous other benefits, such as regulating blood sugar levels in your body, reducing the chance of bingeing/purging, and potentially improving thinking skills too.

Now, to do this I will introduce two different (some may say opposing!) ideas. This is because the nature of your particular difficulties may mean that one is more beneficial than the other. The first is called 'intuitive eating'. This is based on the concept that you are the expert on your own body. The idea is that you should eat when you are hungry and then stop when you are feeling full. This requires an ability to recognize if the feelings or physical sensations you are having are physical hunger sensations, or emotional hunger sensations. This takes time to learn, especially if you have not tuned into the difference between these before.

The second technique is to try and introduce regular eating. You can do this by planning for three meals a day, if this is possible. If it is not, start with just two. On page 193 is a blank meal plan table for you to use, if you wish. Sometimes it helps having a space to plan and write down what you are going to eat, especially if this is something you are not used to doing. I have also included a couple of columns for snacks, if you are able to add these in too.

Blank meal planner

	Meal 1/Breakfast	Snack	Meal 2/Lunch	Snack	Meal 3/Dinner
Monday					
Tuesday					
Wednesday					
Thursday					
Friday					
Saturday					
Sunday					

DOING SOMETHING ABOUT EATING DIFFICULTIES: CHANGING THE ENVIRONMENT

So in this chapter so far you might have completed an eating difficulties journal, a hot cross bun, circles of influence and your stress bucket. From this, you may have been able to begin to make links between certain places, people or things that seem to affect your eating difficulties.

Social media

We know that people on social media usually only show the best bits of their lives, and this can make us feel quite inadequate when looking at all the apparently wonderful things other people are getting up to. We also know that people can often manipulate their photos on social media to change their appearance, which can lead to us comparing ourselves unfairly to something which is not actually real. For some people, making comparisons between their own lives and bodies and the lives and bodies they see presented on social media can lead to certain unhelpful and unhealthy relationships with food, to try and achieve a similar level of 'attractiveness'. First, as I just mentioned, it is worth bearing in mind that people only tend to show the good parts of their lives on social media. What you see is probably the part of their lives they experience maybe 10 per cent of the time. We typically do not get a window into the other 90 per cent of what they do, or what they usually look like. Remember, people can airbrush and edit pictures and photos on social media to give a perception of thinness or an aesthetic that bears no relation to reality. If you recognize that going on social media and making comparisons with other people is part of your difficulty, perhaps limit the amount of time you spend on these sites or apps. Some people find that the best thing to do is just delete their apps altogether. This works for some, but others find social media a great way to connect with others, and this is especially important for Queer people who might not have any other means of engaging with others like them. It might be an idea to try changing the way you use social media to begin with, and instead engaging with body neutral or genuine 'pro-recovery' pages and seeing how this feels. Is it helpful? If so, it might be good to schedule in some specific time each day to visit these pages.

It is important to note that there are social media accounts and websites which are unfortunately designed to promote eating disorders and eating difficulties, so-called 'pro-ana', 'pro-bulimia' or 'pro-mia' pages. These are extremely dangerous and damaging sites and accounts to interact with, and if you come across any of these pages (or perhaps Eddie has told you to look at them) then I encourage you to block or delete them. We know that people visit these sites for many reasons, including feeling heard and understood, which can be very powerful when Eddie can make you feel so isolated. Deleting or blocking these sites may feel very tough if you feel as if they are your only way to be connected to something. But it may feel easier to delete or block them if you find pro-recovery sites, such as those run by eating disorder charities or local eating disorder support groups. There are some resources, links and helplines at the end of this book that will help point you in the right direction.

Distancing yourself from unhelpful people

You may have made links between certain people in your life and the eating difficulties you experience. Perhaps they always seem to be around when you have unhelpful thoughts? Or maybe you always want to engage in certain eating behaviour after a conversation or interaction with them? It is worth considering how beneficial these people are for your mental health and wellbeing. If they are people who are constantly putting you down, commenting on your weight or appearance, or even encouraging you to change the way you eat to obtain a certain look, do you really need to be hanging around with them? It may be useful to look at Chapter 6, *Queer Relationships*, which discusses the impact that relationships can have on our mental health and wellbeing, and provides some activities that you can do to consider what you get from the relationships you have in your life. Do not be afraid to put your own needs first – if others are making your eating difficulties worse, are they the kind of people you want in your life?

Connecting to others

On the flip side, we know that some people use food as a way of fitting in, or dealing with the loneliness that can come from marginalization or rejection. You may have noticed that when you feel alone or disconnected, the eating difficulties tend to become more prominent. Finding someone, or a group of people, that you can relate to and who understand you can be so helpful. One option you could consider is to try out a support group for people who have eating difficulties, and there are some links to charities at the end of this book to help you find local groups in your area. This way of connecting with others may feel a bit safer, especially for Queer people, or Queer people of colour/ Black, Asian, ethnically minoritized/Indigenous/First Nation people, given that we know that having these intersecting identities can make living with eating difficulties tougher to navigate. Connecting with others or making new friends can be so hard, especially as we begin to get older. My main bit of advice here would be: do not be afraid to reach out to others and ask them if they want to meet you for a walk, or coffee, or a chat. Some people will be up for it, others will not. And if others do not want to connect with you, then there could be hundreds of reasons why that are not personal to you (maybe they are a very shy person and struggle themselves with connection?). If you have made friends online or via apps then that is another great way to feel connected to other people, and this type of connection may work for you. Making friends and connections with others is something that takes time, so find what works best for you and be gentle with yourself! There are lots of people out there trying to find connection and trying to fit in too – asking if they want to hang out might just be what they need as well.

SKILLS FROM OTHER SECTIONS THAT MAY BE USEFUL FOR YOU

- Self-compassion skills from Chapter 5, *Self-Acceptance and Self-Compassion*

- Resetting fight or flight from Chapter 8, *Feeling Anxious*

- Safe place imagery from Chapter 8, *Feeling Anxious*

- Low mood skills from Chapter 9, *Feeling Low*

- Creating a self-harm management plan from Chapter 14, *Self-Harm*

- Creating a suicide prevention safety plan from Chapter 15, *Suicide*

SUMMARY

- Eating difficulties can be used for a range of different reasons, and can also be linked to external factors such as poverty and availability of food.

- Specific to some Queer people, unrealistic beauty standards, gender dysphoria and the feelings of not belonging in a heteronormative world can be linked to eating difficulties.

- Tracking eating difficulties using a journal can help us to recognize what seems to be going on before and after we experience this. There may be other factors within the circles of influence that are linked to eating difficulties too.

- Strategies such as recognizing the eating difficulty as a fake and unhelpful friend, talking to other people about this and adding more coping resources to your toolkit can be helpful.

- Distancing yourself from people who encourage maladaptive eating, recognizing if and when social media is helpful and connecting with others are also good things to consider when wanting to change this behaviour.

Space for your own thoughts, reflections, ideas, action plans

Chapter 12

SHAME

Shame can be an incredibly powerful emotion that lots of Queer people experience. It is worth noting that shame and guilt are different emotions. We can experience guilt when we have broken some kind of ethical or moral rule we held dear, such as stealing. So if I walk into a store and steal a chocolate bar, I may feel guilty because I believe that stealing is wrong. Guilt tends to drive us towards somehow making amends. Shame, on the other hand, is different. We can experience shame when we feel as if we have violated some kind of broader, unspoken societal rule or norm. Shame is usually related to our sense of self, rather than any behaviours we may have engaged in. For example, being Queer can carry with it shame because we are violating the unspoken societal norm that is heterosexuality and being cisgender. Whereas guilt can motivate us to correct things, shame can lead to withdrawal and silence.

From an evolutionary perspective, shame and guilt are incredibly powerful emotions. They encourage groups to stick together by situating blame individually. The implication is that if

DID YOU KNOW?

The way that the AIDS pandemic was handled and socially constructed by society was very different from the most recent Covid-19 pandemic. The AIDS pandemic disproportionately affected gay men, and a narrative of this being the 'gay plague' quickly entered the social psyche. Because being gay was constructed by systems and stories as being 'immoral' or 'wrong', public sympathy for those affected by this disease was little-to-none: gay lives were not seen as important enough for accelerated drug treatment trials or top-down government public health initiatives (as we have seen with Covid-19).

Impact on mental health

Gay people were made to believe that what was happening to them was their fault; that they somehow 'deserved' this illness and deserved to die. Negative public responses, family rejection and a campaign of fear led quickly to internalized shame. People who had contracted AIDS were less willing to share this with others, for fear of rejection and public shaming. They often suffered in silence and died alone.

The legacy of the AIDS pandemic still resonates strongly with people today. The idea of gay people being 'dirty' or 'infected' still permeates social narratives, and this can be internalized by gay people. Those who become HIV+ may still believe this to be a death sentence, leading to social and emotional withdrawal, fuelled by the same shame that was bestowed on the community decades earlier. This can lead to numerous self-punishing behaviours, difficulties with mood and feeling out of control.

HIV is not a death sentence, and there are now effective drugs that can prevent exposure. Drugs have also become advanced enough so that routine medication means the amount of HIV someone has in their body is so small, it becomes undetectable. If someone's 'viral load' of HIV is undetectable, they cannot pass HIV onto another *(Undetectable=Untransmittable)*. People living with HIV can live happy, healthy and long lives.

you want to be part of the group for survival, you need to fall in line. Shame and guilt can alert us to the fact that we are not 'falling in line'. This is why shame, in particular, is such a tricky emotional state to manage, because we are made to feel as if we are inherently wrong and do not fit in. This can lead to self-punishing behaviours, withdrawal from others and, for some people, suicidal thoughts.

There are lots of ways that external things around us can lead us to feel shame. People and groups may sideline us for being Queer or make passive-aggressive comments. Some may not be so subtle and instead just actively reject us. Institutions such as religion can be incredibly influential on feelings of shame, perhaps by telling us that a higher power does not approve of our existence. Laws and policies also generate shame if they require you to 'prove' some aspect of yourself, such as your gender identity. And social stories created by a dominant group (such as during the AIDS pandemic when gay people were portrayed by the media as being 'dirty' or 'infected') can have such a far reach that people we love and hold dear may begin to think and behave differently towards us. Sometimes, we identify with this shame and believe it to be true. When this happens, shame becomes internalized.

SHAME WITHIN THE QUEER COMMUNITY

It would be remiss of me to avoid talking about the homo/bi/transphobia that can exist within the Queer community itself. The shame that can be felt from this can be doubly painful, as it is coming from a community of people you thought you were accepted by, or a part of. Queer-shaming behaviours can exist alongside other forms of oppression, such as racism, femmephobia (dislike of femininity), fatphobia (dislike of bigger or larger people), trans-exclusion and toxic masculinity. There is a reason that this exists. And (surprise, surprise) it exists as yet another manifestation of the dominant cishet social story and social norms.

This type of behaviour from Queer people towards other Queer people can perhaps be thought of as 'misdirected bigotry'. What I mean by this is that attacking others who are also oppressed and minoritized can give people a sense of power and control that they may lack in their own lives. This is 'misdirected' because these feelings of anger, unfairness, disgust and rejection actually belong to the cishet world. Yet, because heteronormativity and being cisgender is so pervasive, it can sometimes seem as if these angry feelings have nowhere to go. And firing those feelings towards someone a bit like you can be a way of dealing with internalized homo/bi/transphobia, pushing it onto someone else. In essence, attacking someone else that is a bit like you:

- is easier than trying to dismantle huge, ever-changing, pervasive social and structural systems

- can be a way for some people to manage their own internalized shame.

Ultimately, this maintains our collective oppressed position as Queer people, as the cycle of shame keeps going, and the external things that led us to feel that way in the first place go unchanged. Now the following is important:

This does not mean that shaming, abusive or discriminatory behaviour from one Queer person to another is acceptable. It is not.

My aim here is to bring to your awareness some of the reasons that shame circulates so strongly and can be used as a weapon within both the Queer community and the straight world. Acknowledging what part of this speaks to you and your own experiences is an important first step in recognizing what needs to change. If you have been on the receiving end of shame from within the Queer community, then I also hope that this has helped you externalize *some* of the reasons people may have acted in the way they did. I have said it before, and I will say it again, this does not make what they did right or acceptable. We do not move forward as a community by attacking one another and bringing each other down. We move forward by supporting one another and lifting each other up.

NOTICING WHAT SHAME FEELS LIKE IN YOUR BODY

As with other emotions, shame is likely to make you feel certain things in your body. And similarly, it is good to notice when shame is creeping in by recognizing the bodily sensations it brings with it. This can help us in the future when we are feeling something, but cannot quite put our finger on what it is. Once you can recognize what shame feels like, you know that it is around and you can begin to overcome it.

ACTIVITY

What shame may feel like in your body

Strong urge to run and hide

Defeated, tired, deflated

Blushed cheeks

Feeling sick

Sweaty palms

Feeling hot

What it feels like for me

_____

_____

_____

_____

BEGINNING TO OVERCOME SHAME

Overcoming shame is not easy. If it were, you probably would not be reading this section. That is why I have named this section *beginning* to overcome shame. One thing to highlight before we begin the journey of overcoming shame is to recognize what keeps shame going.

One of the most powerful things that can keep shame going is avoiding the shameful feeling. As humans, we are programmed to avoid things that we do not like, and feeling shame can be a really difficult thing to sit with. So, naturally, people want to try get rid of this feeling as quickly as possible.

Sometimes people will deal with shame by channelling it outwards, away from themselves. This is sometimes why people are angry, aggressive and abusive to others. Other people may avoid this emotion by replacing it with physical pain, as with self-harm. Or they may punish themselves for feeling this way and try to disconnect from this feeling straight away. What tends to happen is that this works for a short time. You may get temporary relief from shameful feelings, though there is an unexpected consequence. What this does is actually *keep the shame going* in the long run. By never sitting with or allowing yourself to feel shame, you allow it to keep its power over you. Next time you feel shame, you are likely to avoid this feeling again, and again, and again. Each time the shameful feelings can become more powerful. So what you need to do is find a way to break this cycle and confront shame, thus reducing the hold it may have over you, and making shame feel less powerful when it creeps in again.

Figure 12.1: The cycle of shame

Figure 12.2: Breaking the cycle of shame: confronting shame and reducing its power

NOTICING AND CONFRONTING SHAME

A potentially good way of managing shame is to notice it and/or confront it. If this is something you have never done before, then it may be especially helpful to externalize it. This means thinking of it as something separate from yourself. For this part of the chapter, I shall present two different techniques you could try. One way in which you can notice shame and slightly distance yourself from it is called *defusion*, a technique from Acceptance and Commitment Therapy (Harris, 2008). The second technique I shall present is called *externalizing* (White & Epston, 1990). I wanted to give two different techniques here because defusion may work for some, and externalizing shame may work for others. Let me take you through an example of how you could apply both these techniques.

We can think of shame as an unwanted visitor – someone who has turned up to the party uninvited. The first thing to do is acknowledge that shame is around.

Defusion	Externalizing
I am noticing that I am having thoughts which are making me feel shame	*Oh look, it is you. Who invited you here?*

Shame is sometimes powerful because it sits in the corner behind other people, looking pretty scary and making us feel some of those physical sensations you identified above. Acknowledging that shame is around this helps us to feel more in control.

Defusion	Externalizing
The thoughts I am having at the moment are a bit like people on a bus – I can hear you all chatting away	*I know you are here, Shame. I can feel a strong urge to run and hide upstairs*

Now, because we know that shame is an emotion that helps us to 'fall in line' and blend into a group, it can make us feel as if we really just want to run away and hide. So, a good way of confronting shame is by refusing to give in to this urge.

Defusion	Externalizing
The thoughts I am having at the moment feel like a bully telling me what to do. I am in charge here, not my thoughts	*Do you know what, Shame, I am not actually going to run away and hide upstairs, as much as I want to, because then you will win. I am going to stay right here*

When you feel shame, I would also encourage you to bring your awareness and attention to your body posture. As with fight or flight, shame can make us automatically change our body posture, so that we are more hunched over, covered or hidden. You may have noticed that you have hidden your face, by turning it away or down. You may have slumped into your chair, or pulled a blanket up to cover yourself. This is because your body is automatically trying to 'hide' you. In order to tell our body that we are safe, and that we do not need to hide ourselves, it is good to make ourselves bigger and more seen. (See 'Doing something about anxiety' in Chapter 8, *Feeling Anxious*, for ways to do this.) If you have covered your face (perhaps by using your hands), then uncover it. If you have slouched down in your chair, stand up. If you have covered your body to hide it, uncover it.

Defusion	Externalizing
I am feeling a real urge to run away and hide because a thought is telling me to. This thought I am having though is no different from a thought about trains – thoughts do not actually have any real power over me	*You want me to hide away and shrink into the background, do not you, Shame? You would like it if I did that, wouldn't you? Well I am not going to*

So far, you have noticed that shame has crept in, you have noticed what physical sensations you have in your body, you are not running away from shame and you are making yourself seen. The final part of confronting shame is to *act opposite* to what shame wants you to do. Shame wants you to avoid it, run away and hide. So, instead, you are going to confront it and take up space. This might not be something you have ever done before, so it may feel quite weird. There are lots of ways to act opposite to shame. The most powerful antidotes to shame involve being seen by others, or by connecting with vulnerability within.

Being seen by others can take lots of forms. This could be just turning up to a party when shame told you to stay home. This could be calling or video-chatting with a friend when shame told you they do not want to talk to you. This could be joining a group or a society when shame told you no one would want you there. A lot of people find performing a great antidote to shame. This could be singing, dancing, drag performing, acting, presenting spoken word or poetry.

Defusion	Externalizing
The thoughts I am having have no power over me, I have power over them. I can choose to engage with these thoughts, or watch them pass, like a train passing through a station	*Stuff you, Shame, I am going to do exactly the OPPOSITE of what you are making me feel! Even though it is scary, I cannot wait to annoy you by singing at the top of my lungs on the karaoke machine! Ha!*

Because shame functions to try and make us hide, there are also ways to connect with vulnerable parts of yourself that shame is trying to force you to hide. Being seen by others is a way of doing this, but you may prefer to do something a little more private. For example, writing is a great way to make sense of your experiences and to give voice to your story. A good way of doing this is to keep a journal or diary, write an online blog (anonymously, if you prefer) or even write letters to the parts of you that feel shameful of, from a compassionate perspective (see *compassionate letter writing* in Chapter 5, *Self-Acceptance and Self-Compassion*). By writing things down, you are allowing the more vulnerable parts of yourself to feel seen, heard and validated.

Defusion	Externalizing
Who is in charge here? I am in charge of my own life, and I am not going to put up with the constant abuse I get from my own thoughts. I am going to imagine putting these thoughts into a box, sealing the box shut and throwing it away	*Shame, you keep telling me that the racism and sexism I received during a lecture was my fault, because I am a Queer, Black woman. But actually, you are wrong, and it was their fault. I am going to write a letter to the part of myself that has had that memory locked away for so long and tell myself that it was not my fault*

The rumination (or worry) that can come with the feeling of shame can be tricky to manage for some people. Thoughts such as 'I should have done things differently' can pop up for some people, so the skills and activities described in Chapter 8, *Feeling Anxious*, may also be helpful for you. The more that you are able to confront shame and act opposite to shameful feelings, the easier it will be to manage. Because we are all human, shame is probably not going to disappear from our lives forever. Rather, we can learn to recognize it, confront it and tell it to get lost when it creeps back in.

SKILLS FROM OTHER SECTIONS THAT MAY BE USEFUL FOR YOU

- Self-compassion skills from Chapter 5, *Self-Acceptance and Self-Compassion*

- Resetting fight or flight from Chapter 8, *Feeling Anxious*

- Observing thoughts and postponing worry from Chapter 8, *Feeling Anxious*

- Acceptance from Chapter 10, *Sleep Difficulties*

- Self-soothe box from Chapter 13, *Trauma*

SUMMARY

- Shame can be a really difficult emotion that serves to make us feel bad for violating group, or societal, rules and norms.

- There are lots of different reasons that Queer people can feel shame, including the social stories that exist around us and influence how other people interact with us.

- The first step to overcoming shame is to notice what it feels like and acknowledge it when it is around.

- Shame can have power over us because we tend to avoid it.

- By confronting shame and acting opposite, we can regain power and control from it.

Space for your own thoughts, reflections, ideas, action plans

— Chapter 13 —

TRAUMA

As we navigate our way through life, things can happen to us that we do not ask for, expect or deserve. Some things we brush off and forget about, and other things stick with us for a long time. These can be singular one-off events, or things that happen repeatedly and over a period of time. These adverse experiences can linger in our minds and, because these memories are so difficult to think about, some people try different strategies to 'get rid' of them. Sometimes we might remember exactly what has happened. Other times, we may have feelings in our bodies and only fragments of memories. Some things that we thought we had brushed off and forgotten about can also suddenly come to mind in certain situations, making the world feel a little less stable, safe and predictable.

The word trauma literally means 'wound'. While this can be a physical wound, it can also take the form of a psychological wound. In the mental health world, we refer to trauma as an experience that was negative, unwanted or difficult to manage, which could have left you feeling that your safety was in danger. Different people will react differently to the same or similar experience. Because of this, it is important to say that other people do not get to decide what is and is not (or was and was not) a traumatic experience for you. If that experience affected you in ways that left you feeling uneasy, upset or threatened, then your experience of that as traumatic is completely valid.

Traumatic events can shape the way that we think, feel, interact with and behave in the world. Because of this, traumatic events can permeate deeply into multiple aspects of our lives. Processing and managing trauma often requires the help of a mental health professional. It is not my aim within this section to engage you in trauma therapy, or to even think about difficult experiences if you do not feel comfortable doing so. Rather, I hope to provide some psychological education around the ways that trauma can affect people. As with other sections, there are some activities and exercises in the pages that follow that you can engage with and complete if you wish. If reading about some of the things I talk about is too difficult or is bringing too many thoughts and feelings up for you all at once, then please skip this chapter and perhaps come back to it later. Please take care of yourself though, and be kind to yourself. I would recommend reading this section in conjunction with the self-compassion part of Chapter 5, *Self-Acceptance and Self-Compassion*, and Chapter 13, *Shame*, because reading about trauma can bring up lots of different emotions and thoughts that can lead us to feelings of shame. Therefore, being kind and compassionate with yourself, and with the reactions or thoughts you have as a result of reading this section, is really important.

TRAUMA AND BEING QUEER

Trauma is something that affects many, many Queer people. For some Queer people, just existing is an ongoing traumatic experience. Because an individual's personal appraisal of an experience determines if it is traumatic for them or not, it is just not possible here to highlight and discuss all the possible events that can be traumatic, and lead to trauma symptoms, for Queer people. What I aim to do, however, is highlight some traumatic experiences that are disproportionately prevalent in the Queer world. I will highlight the most prevalent areas briefly, and I hold my hands up and admit that this will not do justice to the depth of terror, fear and identity crisis that can be associated with such events (they are worthy of books in their own right). So before I go any further, I feel compelled to write the following:

Your existence is valid. You are not disordered. And you are also not to blame for the traumatic events that have happened to you. There is more to you than the trauma you have experienced.

BULLYING

Bullying, at any age, can have a significant effect on a person's self-esteem, confidence and self-worth. Bullying can be overt and obvious; for example, having homo/bi/transphobic slurs said to us, or being publicly shamed because we are Queer. Bullying can also be covert, or subtle. Sometimes this form of bullying is known as 'microaggressions'. This could take the form of exclusion from work/university/school parties, or sarcastic 'compliments' such as 'You are actually OK for a lesbian' (the implication being that in this person's mind most lesbians are not OK, but they will ever so kindly make an exception for you). For some people, when authority figures (e.g., parents or teachers) do not intervene or challenge such discrimination, this can be equally as distressing. This can lead some people to mistrust the ones around them who are supposed to keep them safe.

Sometimes we can sense that something is wrong, but cannot quite put our finger on it. In an interpersonal or group situation, if this is how we are feeling, it could indicate that some form of microaggression is being played out. This can understandably affect our self-esteem or confidence because the people bullying us can make it seem as though we deserve it, or that it is our fault they are targeting us. Sometimes, manipulative bullies can even make us think that we are 'imagining' the bullying, that we are 'just being too sensitive' and that it is actually 'just a joke'. This type of manipulative behaviour is called *gaslighting*, and is a form of psychological abuse.

Bullying can also lead to interpersonal difficulties. Those who have experienced bullying can have issues with trust, connection and intimacy. We may be really sensitive to criticism from others, because critical comments remind us of the time when we were bullied. People who have been bullied may put other people's needs and wishes before their own, because this is how we kept safe and appeased the bullies. Sadly, those of us who have experienced prolonged and extensive bullying may not have a sense of what a relationship feels like, if bullying or abuse do not feature in it. This is why someone may seemingly keep getting into abusive or controlling relationships (romantic or otherwise) – they just might not know any different. Although this type of relationship is not pleasant, it is predictable. As humans, we like predictability as this means we know what to expect and how to handle this.

SEXUAL ASSAULT

Sexual assault can encompass a wide range of assaultive behaviours, including unwanted sexual contact, forced penetration with objects, rape (including marital rape), non-consensual sexual activity and incest. This type of assault can have life-long physical, psychological and emotional consequences, and can be especially traumatic.

For some Queer people, being a survivor of sexual assault can be accompanied by unique difficulties. Some may have been told they 'deserved it' because they are Queer (*NOBODY* deserves to be sexually assaulted), or if the sexual assault was from a man towards another man (or woman towards another woman) then they 'must have enjoyed it' because they are gay (again, *NOBODY* deserves to be sexually assaulted). Some people may struggle to make sense of a sexual assault if they felt sexually aroused during the encounter. Sexual arousal can be common when genitalia are touched, but this is by no means an indicator of 'enjoyment'. Responses to sexual touch can lead to physiological changes, such as an erection or orgasm. Once again, this is not necessarily indicative of enjoyment or pleasure and can be an often automatic bodily process. If a sexual experience was not an activity that all parties had consented to, then this is sexual assault.

Not only can sexual assault have physical implications for someone's body, but it can leave us feeling vulnerable, full of shame and thinking that it was our fault. This can impact on future sexual experiences. Some Queer people can end up finding it tricky knowing where the boundaries of consent for sexual activity lie, especially if we were made to feel that the sexual abuse we experienced was our fault. In the box below is an explanation of consent that I think is pretty helpful, using the metaphor of a cup of tea.

CONSENT FOR SEXUAL ACTIVITY – THE CUP OF TEA ANALOGY

A memorable way to think of consent is using the analogy of a cup of tea. You can choose to drink tea today, and then choose coffee tomorrow and that is OK. You can make yourself a cup of tea right now, and then decide not to drink it. You can start walking towards the kettle and turn it on, and then decide to not make a cup of tea. You could also begin drinking your cup of tea and then decide to put it down and stop drinking it. Other people can offer you tea, and you can accept or refuse. Even if you accept someone's invitation for tea, you can change your mind and say 'no thanks' when they have started boiling the kettle.

Think of this cup of tea as sexual activity. You can choose to engage in sex, and then change your mind. You can be mid-way through sexual activity, and choose to stop. Other people can offer you sex, and you can say no.

If someone forces you to drink tea when you do not want to, or makes you feel uncomfortable while you are drinking tea, then this is *not* OK. If someone forces you to engage in sexual activity when you do not want to, or makes you feel uncomfortable while you are engaged in sexual activity, then this is *not* OK, and is no longer consensual sex. There are specialist sexual violence charities that can support you if you have engaged in non-consensual sex. There are also specially trained officers within the police service who can support you if you wish to report this. Any report of sexual abuse, including rape, should be handled with the utmost respect and privacy. You can, and will be, supported throughout this process. Links and helplines are available at the end of this book.

RELIGIOUS/CULTURAL TRAUMA

It should be made clear that not all religions or faith systems are punitive and punishing of Queer people. At the heart of most religious teachings is the message of love. Religion can be hugely important for some Queer people, and their relationship with a higher spiritual being can be incredibly comforting.

Particularly relevant for some Queer people is the impact of religious or cultural trauma. Within some religious communities, being Queer is thought of as resulting from demonic possession, or witchcraft. While this narrative (and the subsequent shame that may be felt) is traumatic in and of itself, subsequent rituals or cultural practices that can follow to try and 'cleanse' the Queer person can be torturous and extremely traumatic. In case you are reading this book and are not aware, being 'cleansed' or physically assaulted as a result of religious beliefs or ideology is *abuse*, and I would encourage you to seek support in reporting it to the authorities.

Furthermore, within some religions or cultures there may be the practice of arranged marriage. This is usually when parents decide whom their child will marry. The assumption is that if you are a man you will marry a woman and vice versa. If you do not identify with your sex assigned at birth, or you are anything but heterosexual, I imagine that this can be an utterly isolating and shameful experience. Often the power of the family structure, religious or cultural community, and worry about bringing 'shame' on the family forces the individual to comply with the marriage. The result for some is years of mood difficulties, identity crisis ('Am I really Queer?', 'How can I be if I am now married to a man/woman?') and self-defeating behaviours.

PHYSICAL AND EMOTIONAL ABUSE

Physical assault can be a very traumatic experience, and can occur alongside bullying, sexual assault and religious/cultural trauma. Put simply, if someone physically does something to you without your permission or consent, this is physical assault. This can range from someone spitting at you, to punching or kicking you, to forcing you to engage in some kind of 'treatment' or ritual. When this happens, our sense of safety is seriously compromised, and understandably our fight or flight response will kick in.

Physical assault can fall under the category of domestic violence. This is violence of any kind within the household. Domestic violence is just as prevalent within the Queer community as it is in the cishet community, though social stories about Queer people and expected rejection or prejudice from authorities can make it difficult for Queer people to report it. There are domestic abuse helplines at the end of this book if you need to reach out for support.

Just like physical abuse, emotional abuse is likely to be associated with all the different types of traumatic experience I have discussed so far. This can take the form of the survivor being told they deserved it (they did not), or that they caused the other person to get angry (we are all responsible for our own individual actions). Physical assault (especially within domestic violence) can sometimes be accompanied by remorse from the abuser. They may tell you afterwards that they 'did not mean it' and they 'still love you'. This form of emotional abuse serves to keep you quiet, keep you within the relationship, and make you believe that the abuse you are experiencing is not too bad (*any* abuse is bad and not acceptable). By its very definition, homo/bi/transphobia is emotional abuse as it can lead a Queer person to feel bad for simply existing.

For trans people, one form of emotional abuse may be the repeated use of their 'dead name' by others. A 'dead name' is the name associated with their previous identity, or previous life. This can be incredibly traumatic for trans people, and abusers are likely to be aware of this. People may think that calling someone by their dead name is funny, or that they are just 'having a laugh'. This can be incredibly painful for some trans people who associate this with an identity they do not want to be reminded of. There is a big difference in someone using a trans person's dead name accidentally, and doing so purposefully, and to do this constitutes emotional abuse. It is absolutely worth saying that even accidental dead-naming can be extremely painful (especially from loved ones) and that it is OK to feel hurt even if someone has not overtly meant offence. The same goes for misgendering. If someone identifies with certain pronouns or with a certain gender, and people purposefully use incorrect pronouns or their incorrect gender identity, this can feel incredibly hurtful and is emotionally abusive.

HEALTHCARE TRAUMA

For some Queer people, seeking help from medical professionals and institutions can be a traumatic experience. This may not be the first thing that springs to mind when we think of 'trauma', but it is a common experience that many Queer people report. I am, of course, not suggesting or implying that all healthcare professionals or services are inherently traumatic. In fact, I know many who are the kindest people I have ever met. However, to avoid this topic risks avoiding a trauma that many Queer people have experienced and continue to experience.

An example of this is the practice of 'conversion therapy'. This 'therapy' (which it is not) is used to apparently 'convert' someone to a heterosexual and/or cisgender way of life. Conversion therapy is totally unscientific, completely immoral and unethical, and has no evidence to support it. The experience of conversion therapy can leave deep psychological wounds as the individual is made to feel that the very core of their existence is wrong.

For trans people, seeking help for gender dysphoria (the feeling of discomfort that your sex assigned at birth differs from the gender you identify with) can be a traumatic experience. Trans people in some countries (such as the UK) are placed on hugely lengthy waiting lists to be assessed. After this, there is usually a significant amount of time where the trans person is expected to demonstrate that the gender they identify with is 'really what they want'. This can take the form of 'presenting' as this gender for a period of time, before beginning hormone replacement therapy. Frequent thoughts such as 'Do I pass for this gender?' or 'Am I masculine/feminine enough?' can of course lead to intense feelings of anxiety (particularly in social situations). This prolonged process can be incredibly distressing, as the person may feel as if the medical professional they are seeing is denying the validity of their existence. Furthermore, I imagine that there is a huge amount of shame and vulnerability that comes with someone else making *literally life-changing* decisions about you. It is therefore no wonder that some people, as a result of this process, can experience loss of social relationships, and difficulties with body image or with regulating their feelings.

For Queer people accessing sexual health services, this can also carry with it prejudice and punitive responses from some healthcare professionals. For example, Queer people may be told that they need to 'rein in their sexually promiscuous behaviour' if they are repeatedly getting sexually transmitted diseases. Or a lesbian may be questioned by doctors as to why they are not on contraception (because the dominant heteronormative social story is that women must be straight and must want to have children, alongside the assumption that it is the woman's burden to use contraception!). While this may be appropriate clinical advice, the way that this is delivered is of utmost importance. If this is delivered in a shaming, judgemental and critical way, the Queer person receiving this can feel humiliated. This can also make them resistant to reaching out for medical support in the future, if this is how they think they will be treated.

THE IMPACT OF TRAUMA

Because there are many different traumatic experiences, and it can be unique to a specific person, trauma can impact us in many ways. It can lead to unwanted or unhelpful thoughts, nightmares, intrusive memories, flashbacks, a hyperactive fight or flight response, hearing distressing voices that other people cannot hear or seeing distressing things that other people cannot see. Trauma can run deep, like the roots of a tree in soil. If we think of ourselves as a tree, then traumatic roots (things that have happened to us such as adverse childhood or community experiences) can lead to a weakened or unstable trunk (unhelpful thoughts, an unstable sense of self, reduced self-compassion), leading to branches and leaves that can easily break (intense emotions, self-harm, substance use). This visual depiction of trauma is known as the 'trauma tree'. Here is an example:

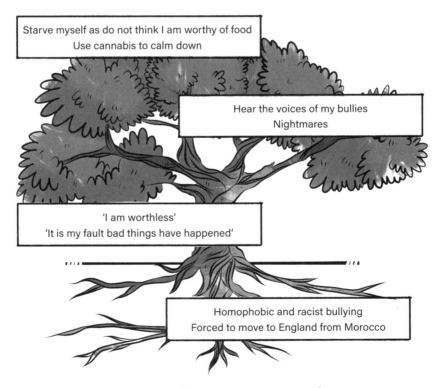

Starve myself as do not think I am worthy of food
Use cannabis to calm down

Hear the voices of my bullies
Nightmares

'I am worthless'
'It is my fault bad things have happened'

Homophobic and racist bullying
Forced to move to England from Morocco

Figure 13.1: The trauma tree: an example

In this trauma tree example, this person has moved to England from Morocco, where they experienced homophobia and racism growing up. This led to beliefs about themselves that they are worthless and that what happened to them was their fault. As a result, they are hearing the voices of their bullies in their head, and having nightmares. To manage this, they are using cannabis to calm down and are starving themselves because they do not think they are worthy of food. This person has been through some really distressing and horrible experiences, so it is no wonder they feel the way they do. What happened to them is, of course, not their fault at all, but because they were led to believe that being Queer was wrong, they have internalized this sense of worthlessness and feel as if they deserve bad things happening to them.

I hope from the above example you can see how early experiences shape the way we think, which can in turn lead to experiences and feelings that are difficult to manage. We may engage in certain behaviours to try and manage them. If it is helpful, and you want to try and make some of the links between things that have happened to you, there is a blank trauma tree on the following page. Take this exercise slowly if you do explore this. It will be helpful to consult Chapter 5, *Self-Acceptance and Self-Compassion*, after you have completed this exercise, if it was particularly difficult for you. There are other some activities for you to try in this section to manage any difficult emotions you may have.

ACTIVITY

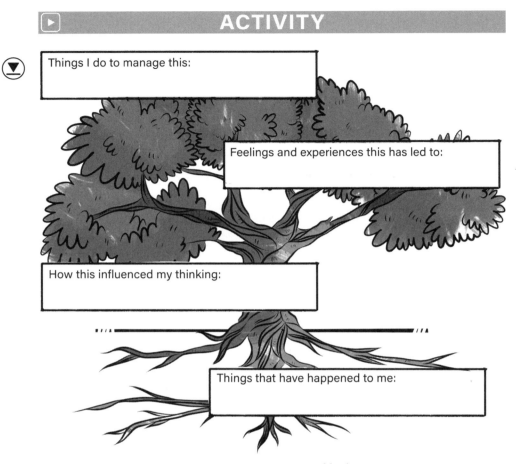

Things I do to manage this:

Feelings and experiences this has led to:

How this influenced my thinking:

Things that have happened to me:

Figure 13.2: The trauma tree: blank copy

USING SUBSTANCES TO MANAGE

People manage trauma in lots of different ways. They may use physiological strategies to calm or regulate their bodies. Some people who have experienced trauma may use medication prescribed by a doctor to manage this. Others may self-medicate and use legal and illegal substances to manage their distress. This could be nicotine, alcohol, prescription drugs or recreational drugs. People often self-medicate for a variety of reasons, including to numb difficult feelings (including anxiety), to help 'forget' or distract themselves from intrusive or traumatic memories/images, and to punish themselves.

This tends to work for a short while, although there are often lots of difficulties associated with this way of coping, including mental health, financial, social and health implications. Addiction may be the result of repeated use of a particular substance. This means that the body has become reliant on using this substance and it can be difficult for the individual to function without it. If an individual stops using a particular substance, they can experience a physiological reaction known as 'withdrawal'. This makes it difficult to resist using the substance, and the substance is now used to stop these withdrawal effects. The individual can then get caught up in a cycle of using substances. They can feel bad when they are using them as they 'know they should not' and bad when they are not using them because of withdrawal symptoms and difficult-to-manage emotions. This same principle applies for other addictive behaviours that may serve similar functions for managing trauma, such as a sex, gambling, binge eating or porn addiction.

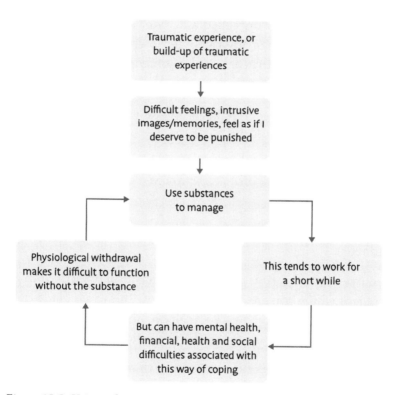

Figure 13.3: Using substances to manage trauma: unintended consequences

Because of this strong physiological component, I would highly recommend that you consult a medical professional if you wish to stop using any kind of substance. This is because if you stop suddenly you may experience strong withdrawal effects. For this reason, people usually have to detox from substances in a controlled way, under medical supervision.

I would strongly encourage you to first try using skills from this book to manage your feelings, and seek mental health support. If, however, you have been using substances for a little while and want to know how to do this more safely, the tips below may help. These tips do not constitute medical advice and you should discuss your substance use with your doctor or medical professional as soon as possible, so that they can help you out. You could discuss (or practise) having this conversation with a dedicated LGBTQ+ helpline (listed at the end of the book):

- If you inject substances, always ensure you use a clean needle. Some services will offer needle exchange programmes so you can swap a used needle for a clean one, no questions asked.

- Use substances in a controlled and safe environment. For example, try and use these near other people, so you can get help if you need to. If this is not possible, at least let someone know where you are and what you are using.

- Always measure out or weigh the substances you are using so you do not accidentally overdose.

- Ensure that you know what is in the substances you are using. 'Street drugs' can often have other substances mixed in with them that can be lethal.

- Linking to the above point, buy substances from someone you know and trust.

- Remove any dangerous or potentially harmful objects from the environment where you are using substances. This can include things that you could fall over and hurt yourself on, or objects that you might use to hurt yourself if you were under the influence.

- Try using a little less of the substance than you usually would. If, for example, you usually drink a bottle of vodka, try pouring a little bit out before you start drinking so you do not drink the whole thing. If you take pills, try taking one or two fewer.

WHEN THE MIND AND BODY THINK WE ARE IN DANGER AGAIN: GROUNDING TECHNIQUE

Sometimes when people have experienced traumatic things, they can feel a bit disconnected from reality, as if things around them do not always feel real. This is something our bodies can do to help us manage overwhelming memories and feelings. Sometimes people experience flashbacks or intrusive memories, which make them feel as if the traumatic experience is happening all over again, right in that moment. These experiences can be really scary. To help with this, try to reconnect with the here-and-now. Tell your mind and body that these things are not happening all over again. This is called grounding yourself, and exercises that help you do this are known as *grounding techniques*. This is basically a strategy to help convince your body that you are safe. A good way to do this is to engage all five senses.

The first thing to do is recognize when you usually feel slightly disconnected, or when an intrusive memory or image usually comes along. A good way to do this is to recognize triggers. If you wanted to learn more about your triggers for this particular experience, I would recommend using the mood diaries introduced in Chapter 8, *Feeling Anxious*. You can use these diaries exactly as they are. Just replace 'Mood I want to track' at the top with 'Intrusive memory/image, or disconnected feeling I want to track'.

ACTIVITY

When you notice that you are feeling a little disconnected from what is going on around you, or that an unwanted memory or image has popped into your head, first:

Name five things you can see

This can be anything in the environment around you. Some people find it useful just to focus on one part of their environment rather than looking all around, until they feel more grounded.

Then:

Name four things you can hear

What can you hear around you? Are there people or animals? A TV or radio? A drilling noise outside or the sound of your fish tank?

After this:

Name three things you can touch or feel

A good thing to start with is feeling the ground beneath your feet, or if you are sitting down, your bottom against whatever surface you are sitting on. If you are on a soft surface like a bed, some people report that it is helpful moving to a harder surface (like the floor) to feel more grounded.

Now:

Name two things that you can smell

If you are outside, can you smell any flowers or freshly cut grass? What does the breeze smell like? If you are inside, can you smell any candles or diffusers, food, or even the fragrance or perfume you might be wearing?

Finally:

Name one thing that you can taste

This one can be a little odd, especially if you are not eating anything! If there is food or drink close by, have a bite or a sip and notice what this tastes like. Maybe you have some gum or mints in your pocket you could chew or suck. If there is nothing available, just notice if there is any kind of taste or sensation in your mouth.

It is best to practise this grounding technique when you feel relatively grounded, so that it is easier to do when you feel a bit more disconnected. For the next activity, I will walk you through how to create a 'self-soothe' box. This box also focuses on the five senses, so to make this grounding technique easier, it might be good to carry some things around with you from your self-soothe box to help you smell, taste and feel things.

SELF-SOOTHE BOX

A great resource that has roots in Dialectical Behaviour Therapy is the self-soothe box (sometimes also called an emotional first aid kit or emotional bug out bag). This is a collection of items that are comforting, soothing, self-compassionate and relaxing, that can be used in times of stress. So, when you are feeling intense emotions, have awoken from a nightmare, are hearing distressing voices or seeing distressing things that other people cannot, or are having intrusive memories, a self-soothe box is a great way to ground yourself and immerse yourself in things you enjoy. The great thing about creating a self-soothe box is that it can be completely personalized to you. There is no 'right' or 'wrong' thing to put in, and your self-soothe box can be as big or as small as you like.

The physical box itself could, for example, be a shoebox or plastic container. Feel free to get creative – decorate your box with wrapping paper, stickers, your favourite people or whatever arts and crafts you like. Next, is the fun part – filling the box! Anything and everything that is soothing or comforting can go in: your favourite sweets or chocolate, your favourite perfume, bubble wrap, pictures of your favourite people/memories, stones you have collected, your favourite book...the possibilities are endless! I would encourage you to include things in the box that involve the five senses. So think about things that are nice to look at, smell, touch, taste and hear. It is good to find something small that you can keep in your pocket too, as a portable self-soothe item. Below are some examples of what you could include from each of these five categories.

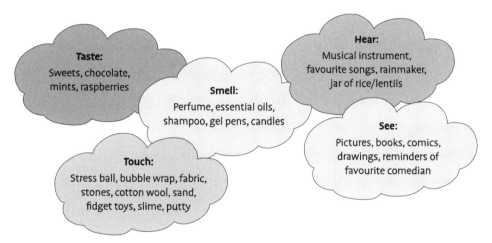

Figure 13.4: Things to include in my self-soothe box

ACTIVITY

What I could put in my self-soothe box:

Things I like to touch:

_____

_____

Things I like to taste:

_____

_____

Things I like to smell:

_____

_____

Things I like to hear:

_____

_____

Things I like to see:

_____

_____

TIPP SKILL

Another great Dialectical Behaviour Therapy skill for managing distressing or intense emotions is the TIPP skill. TIPP stands for Temperature, Intense exercise, Paced breathing and Paired muscle relaxation. It is a good, simple acronym to remember when you need to call on some skills quickly to help you regulate how you are feeling.

ACTIVITY

Temperature

A great way to quickly calm down is by putting your face into a bowl of very cold water for 20–30 seconds (or however long you can safely do this for). This activates something called the mammalian dive reflex, a natural reflex that all mammals (including humans) have. We can activate this in humans by putting our face into cold water. The way this reflex works is that our heart rate slows down and our parasympathetic nervous system activates a 'relaxation' response. This can leave us feeling calmer, and can take the intensity out of difficult emotions. You do not have to submerge your face in water if you do not want to. You could also place something cold on your face (such as a bag of peas, or ice cubes wrapped in a towel) or put your face under a cold shower (though not for too long!).

ACTIVITY

Intense exercise

Exercising can release endorphins, chemicals that the body releases to combat stress. Doing short bursts of intense exercise can be a great way to manage difficult feelings and experiences. For example, you could sprint for a short time outside, jog intensely on the spot, or do some push-ups or squats. Some people also like to channel some of their difficult feelings into exercise, by hitting a punchbag for example.

Something important to bear in mind with this skill is that you should try and be aware of the function of your intense exercise. If it is to regulate intense emotions with the aim of making you feel calmer, then that is OK. However, if you are aware that you have a tricky relationship with exercise (perhaps you use exercise as a way of punishing yourself, or to burn calories as part of difficulties with eating), or are unable to exercise (e.g., you may have a disability that prevents you from doing so), then I would suggest skipping this and focusing on some other skills instead.

ACTIVITY

Paced breathing

Similar to the breathing exercise in Chapter 8, *Feeling Anxious*, paced breathing is a technique to help us regulate breathing and heart rate. As before, this involves taking more time on the out breath than on the in breath. The way to do this is to find somewhere comfortable to sit, and breathe deeply in through your nose for four seconds (this is sometimes referred to as 'abdominal breathing'). Then, slowly breathe out through your mouth for six seconds. Repeat this for a minute or two, and notice how much calmer you feel. If you do not feel calmer after this, do not worry. This technique may not be especially useful for you, so try something else.

 ACTIVITY

Paired muscle relaxation

Information on paired muscle relaxation can be found in Chapter 8, *Feeling Anxious* ('Untensing your muscles'). This exercise is about focusing on parts of your body. Those people who struggle with body dysmorphia (worrying about the appearance of different parts of your body) or gender dysphoria may find it more beneficial to skip this and try one of the other exercises.

HOPE AND GROWTH AFTER TRAUMA

Reading this chapter back to myself, I realize that the things I have talked about, and the ways that people often manage these experiences, can perhaps paint a pretty bleak picture of living with trauma. As mentioned at the very start of this chapter, trauma can filter through into multiple aspects of our lives and change the way that we interact with the world. While this can be incredibly debilitating and distressing, it is worth mentioning that some people can, and do, experience hope and growth when difficult and traumatic things have happened to them. For example, when people begin to understand and believe that the things that happened to them were not their fault, they may realize that they themselves are not 'faulty' as humans and they did what they did to manage living in this messy world. The relief that this can bring to some should not be underestimated. Some people also describe a new-found passion for activism, charity work or volunteering after they have experienced trauma or adversity. There are also some who reflect on the relationships they have in their lives and the values they hold dear, and start to re-evaluate how these fit with their desired goals and life direction.

Talking about hope and change after trauma is important, because it can help people to understand that trauma does not have to define you, and that you can still live a fulfilling life despite what has happened to you. What I should make clear though, is that experiencing hope and growth after traumatic experiences is not what always happens. Indeed, for many just waking up the next morning is all that matters, and to these people I say *that is more than enough*. You do not need to change life direction or have a new-found philosophy on life to validate your trauma. Surviving and breathing is enough, for today.

SKILLS FROM OTHER SECTIONS THAT MAY BE USEFUL FOR YOU

- Self-compassion skills from Chapter 5, *Self-Acceptance and Self-Compassion*

- Resetting fight or flight from Chapter 8, *Feeling Anxious*

- Safe place imagery from Chapter 8, *Feeling Anxious*

- Low mood skills from Chapter 9, *Feeling Low*

- Creating a self-harm management plan from Chapter 14, *Self-Harm*

- Creating a suicide prevention safety plan from Chapter 15, *Suicide*

SUMMARY

- Trauma is unique to an individual, and can be a single event or a build-up of events over time.

- Being Queer can mean that people may have experienced traumatic events such as bullying, sexual or physical assault, religious trauma or healthcare trauma.

- Trauma can affect us deeply, influencing our thoughts, feelings and behaviours.

- Strategies such as grounding, creating a self-soothe box or using the TIPP skill can be useful ways of managing some of the responses we have to trauma.

- Some people may use substances to manage trauma, but this can sometimes have problematic consequences, and advice should be sought from a medical professional.

Space for your own thoughts, reflections, ideas, action plans

— Chapter 14 —

SELF-HARM

WHAT IS SELF-HARM, AND WHY DO PEOPLE DO IT?

When people refer to 'self-harm' they most often think of someone who hurts their own body in ways that are visible, such as by cutting, burning or scratching themselves. While this is a form of self-harm, self-harm can be thought of as a broader category of self-defeating and punishing behaviours aimed at hurting yourself physically and/or psychologically. For example, although drinking excessive alcohol or restricting food intake would not be captured within the 'medical definition' of self-harm, they can be forms of self-harm if they are being used as a way of punishing yourself. Furthermore, engaging in risky sexual behaviour (such as unprotected sex or sexual behaviour while under the influence of substances) can also be a form of self-harm, again if the function of this is to intentionally hurt yourself for some reason. Self-harm and suicide are different things, although someone can be engaging in self-harm as well as suicidal behaviours. Self-harming behaviours are, paradoxically, described by some people as a way of keeping them alive by providing them with a strategy they can use to manage their overwhelming feelings.

Self-harm is a common behaviour within the Queer community, and we now know this is particularly the case when it comes to non-suicidal self-injury for bisexual people (Dunlop *et al.*, 2020). We know that people start hurting themselves for a wide variety of reasons, and some of these may be connected to being Queer. For example,

> **Self-harm can include:**
> Disordered, restricted or binge eating
> Non-suicidal self-injury (e.g., cutting, burning, scratching, inserting objects into the skin)
> Excessive substance use
> Risky sexual behaviour

something may happen to us that leaves us feeling lots of overwhelming emotions. This could be an assault, an experience of intense shame or the build-up of lots of minority stress. Someone may find that certain self-harming behaviours allow them to now have a sense of control over what happened to them, and to regulate how they are feeling. This can be such an effective strategy at meeting a particular need, such that over time we learn and remember that self-harm worked when something difficult happened.

The potential for self-harm to help us feel better in the short term could actually apply to lots of people – just because you use this way of coping does not mean there is anything 'abnormal' about you. Self-harm provides distraction from internal states; it shifts attention from what can be unmanageable emotional pain to manageable physical pain. This means that in the future, if something else happens that is tough to deal with, we may automatically choose self-harm before considering other options. Usually, however, there are lots of barriers to self-harm, such as a positive view of ourselves. When these barriers are eroded or chipped away, which happens a lot with Queer people for a variety of reasons, we are much more likely to use self-harm as a coping strategy (Hooley & Franklin, 2018). This then keeps the self-harming cycle going, because we do not always consider other things that could help us instead, and default to this method of coping.

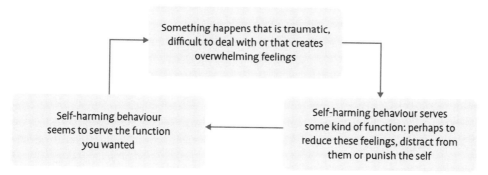

Figure 14.1: The cycle of self-harm

Even though self-harm at some point worked for a particular difficulty, it can have consequences we might not have thought about. While self-harm may help with difficult feelings in the short term, this does not resolve the underlying problem. People who hurt themselves can be left with physical reminders, such as self-harm scarring, extreme weight loss/gain or infections. This can end up having an impact on someone's body image and confidence. These physical effects of self-harm can themselves be very difficult to deal with. What once was a solution can then become part of the problem.

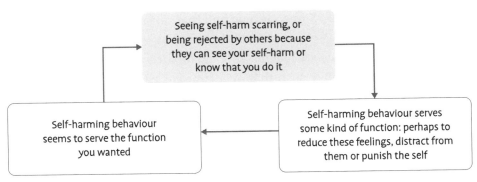

Figure 14.2: The cycle of self-harm: when what felt like
the solution becomes part of the problem

At this stage some people may think about getting some help. As mentioned in Chapter 13, *Trauma*, for some Queer people, their experiences of seeking help from healthcare professionals or institutions can be traumatic. Seeking help for self-harming behaviours can feel really tough, because social stigma and stories exist that make this particularly difficult to share. So when this is coupled with any other difficult or traumatic experiences (such as previous Queer-related discrimination or stigma), this can make asking for help for self-harm even tougher.

You would think that if a person goes to their GP or the emergency department and tells someone about their self-harming behaviours, they clearly want help. However, there seems to be a very strong social story that people who hurt themselves are 'attention-seeking'. Because of this, people may respond to individuals who self-harm in an unhelpful and unkind way. Unhelpful responses can include people telling you to 'just stop doing it' (I mean, if it were as simple as that, I am sure you would have already done that by now?!). If someone has a negative experience of care when they seek help, this can invalidate the courage it has taken to reach out for support, and potentially bring about feelings of shame. People learn that self-harm is not something they can talk about with others as they do not take it seriously. This is another cycle that can sometimes keep self-harming behaviour going.

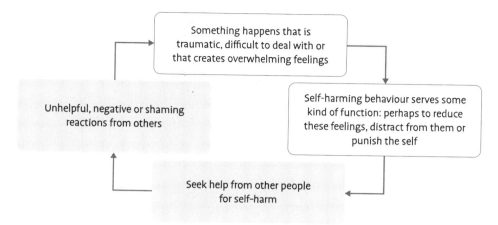

Figure 14.3: The cycle of self-harm: when unhelpful reactions from others make things worse

Table 14.1: Common myths and assumptions about self-harm

Myth or assumptions	The reality
Self-harm is about attention-seeking	While self-harm may be a way to communicate distress to another person, there is usually much more going on than just trying to 'get attention'
People who self-harm want to die	Quite the opposite. People who self-harm often say that they do it to manage everyday life. It is described by some as a way of actually keeping them alive
People who self-harm are dangerous to others	Often the only person who is in danger when it comes to self-harm is the person who is doing this to themselves
People who self-harm must have a mental health difficulty	Self-harm is a coping strategy used by many, many people. Some people who self-harm may experience mental health difficulties, some may not

MOVING AWAY FROM SELF-HARM

What I am not going to do in this chapter is preach to you about why you should stop self-harming immediately. We know that this does not work! Self-harming behaviour serves a function for people, and may often have been one of the only coping or survival strategies they had, or have. So to ask someone to stop this immediately, without giving them any skills or strategies to do things differently, is not helpful. I guess the only caveat to this is if the self-harm behaviour is immediately life-threatening and poses imminent risk of death or serious illness (e.g., ligaturing or 'self-strangulation'). If this is the case, then such behaviour should be stopped and replaced with something less damaging as a matter of urgency. If you feel that you cannot control any life-threatening self-harm, and want help to stop doing it, please call emergency services on 999 in the UK, 112 in Europe and 911 in the USA.

In this chapter we are, instead, going to work together to build a 'managing my self-harm' plan. To do this, I am going to help you explore what the urge to self-harm feels like for you in the first place. Then, I am going to help you to think about why you may be self-harming, by tracking this over time using a diary. Once you know why you may be self-harming, and what the urge to self-harm feels like, this gives you an opportunity to try something different instead. So, we will then look at things that you can try doing when the urge is weak, when the urge feels stronger and when the urge feels unmanageable.

Let us be real – this is not going to solve things instantly! Rather, I hope you can see this as the beginning of change. Things you try may not work very well for you, so you may want to think again about trying something different. As with other difficulties, I would ultimately encourage you to try and seek help from a mental health professional. If you do seek help from someone, you can share your management plan with them, and perhaps they will have other ideas you can try. Some parts of the next few pages have numbers next to them. You can ignore these for now (they are needed later).

THE URGE TO SELF-HARM

A lot of people who hurt themselves say that they can feel it coming on, almost as if they have an urge to do it. Some say the urge kind of feels a bit like an itch that needs to be scratched, or like a sneeze that is coming. You know it is going to happen; you are just waiting for it. Even though these urges can feel inevitable, there are ways of managing them. Everyone's urges can feel different, and when you are reading this you may have an idea of what your urge to self-harm feels like. In the box on the following page, it may be useful to write down what your urge to self-harm can feel like. There may be multiple things that you feel, or certain feelings associated with different self-harm behaviours. Just make a note of any connections or links between certain situations/people/things, specific urges and specific self-harming behaviour.

ACTIVITY

What an urge to self-harm may feel like in your body

Tense muscles
Increased heart rate
Restlessness or shakiness
Sick feeling
A 'hot rush' or 'hot flush'
Like an 'itch' on the skin

What it feels like for me

_____

_____

_____

_____

If you think back to Chapter 3, *Queer Mental Health: The Basics*, I introduced the idea that thoughts, feelings and behaviours can be connected. Because of this, some people notice that there are certain thoughts they get before they self-harm. These could include thoughts about coping (e.g., 'I cannot cope' or 'Everything feels overwhelming') or thoughts about punishing themselves ('I am a bad person' or 'Why do I have to be so stupid?'). Some studies also suggest that mental imagery is common before self-harm, such as images of the act itself or of the injury. To help you understand some more about why you may be hurting yourself, it is also good to note any thoughts that you remember having when you have previously self-harmed. You can write these in the box on the following page. Do not worry if you cannot think of any for now, we will come back to this.

ACTIVITY

1 **Thoughts that I have before I self-harm:**

Below is an image of an 'urge thermometer'. We are going to use this to help you to track the intensity of your urges, and also when it comes to making your 'managing my self-harm' plan. As you can see, the thermometer goes from 1 to 10. The number 1 represents an urge that is noticeable, but that you feel fully in control of. By contrast, 10 represents an urge that is feeling really unmanageable. There is also a blank urge thermometer for you to write down any physical sensations or thoughts that go through your head at various points on the urge thermometer.

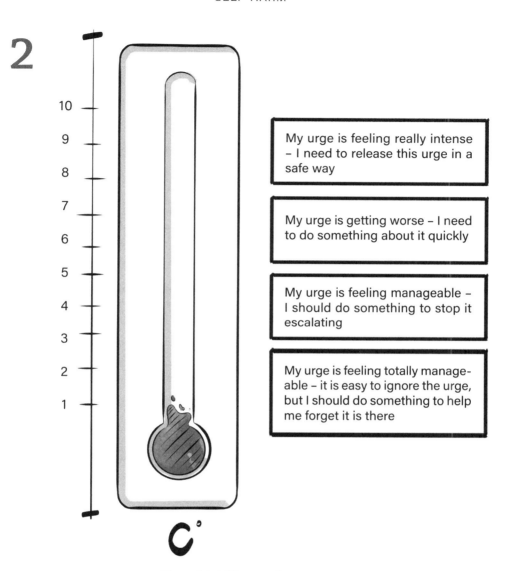

Figure 14.4: The urge themometer

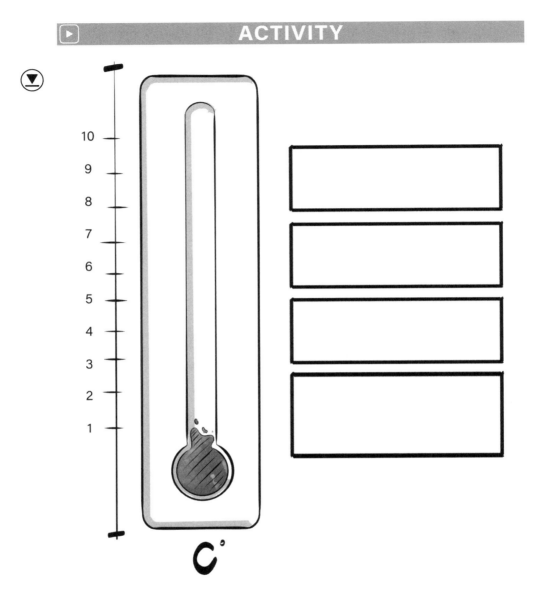

Figure 14.5: The blank urge themometer

TRACKING URGES AND SELF-HARM: USING A DIARY

Getting urges to self-harm can sometimes be associated with certain people, places, activities or mood states. The way we can learn more about our urges to self-harm, as well as the function that self-harming behaviour may serve for us, is to track them using a diary. On the following page is an example of the type of thing that you can write under each section.

Table 14.2: Example diary for tracking self-harming urges

What number was my urge on the thermometer?	Where was I? What time was it? Who was I with?	What was going on just before I got the urge?	What thought(s) went through my head?	What did I feel emotionally and/ or in my body?	How did I manage the urge?	What did I feel afterwards?
5	At home in my bedroom, it was 8pm	My abusive ex-partner messaged me	'What if they come to find me?'	Panic, stress, hands sweaty, lots of feelings	I called my friend to tell them and then watched a film to distract myself	Slightly calmer but took a little while, and also pleased with myself that I did not scratch myself
9	In bed, midnight, just about to fall asleep	Ex-partner tried to call me	'I cannot do this' 'They are going to hurt me again'	Panic, terror, shame, self-disgust	I scratched myself	Calmer, less disgusted with myself

From this example, you can see that this person had a few urges in the same night. The urge to hurt themselves seemed to come just after this person received contact from an abusive ex-partner. Understandably, they felt scared and panicky because of this contact. The first time this happened the urge was manageable, and this person was able to call their friend and distract themselves. This made them feel calmer, though it was a little while until they felt calm. The second time they got this urge it was much stronger, and they scratched themselves. This also made them feel calmer.

When we look closely at what they felt emotionally, they were feeling shame and self-disgust. It would be interesting and useful for this person to keep tracking their self-harming urges and behaviour for a few more weeks to see if self-harm always seems to happen after they feel strong feelings of shame and self-disgust. If it does, then this is an important link. This can help the person realize that when they feel those strong feelings they have really strong urges to self-harm, so they can try to do something else instead. Also, it seems pretty clear that this person's ex-partner is a trigger for their strong feelings. This also gives an opportunity for change – can this person block their ex-partner from messaging them? Removing triggers is a good way to manage urges. We will come on to this later. On the following page is a blank diary that you may find useful to complete. I would suggest tracking your self-harming urges for a week or two, so you can capture lots of relevant information. This is because different things may be associated with different urges. If you get lots of urges every day, then you may only need to track your urges for a few days in order to get an idea of your triggers.

1 Blank self-harming urge diary

What number was my urge on the thermometer?	Where was I? What time was it? Who was I with?	What was going on just before I got the urge?	What thought(s) went through my head?	What did I feel emotionally and/or in my body?	How did I manage the urge?	What did I feel afterwards?

HOT CROSS BUN AND CIRCLES OF INFLUENCE FOR SELF-HARM

You may have read through some other sections of this book and come across the hot cross bun and circles of influence before. If you have not, and want to learn more, I would recommend going to Chapter 3, *Queer Mental Health: The Basics*. The reason I have included it here is that some of you reading this may be familiar with this way of thinking about difficulties now. You may find it more helpful to complete this activity rather than (or in addition to) the self-harming urge diary. This may be especially helpful if you already know quite a lot about the triggers for your self-harm and want to see how these are externally influenced by other people and groups, institutions, laws and policies and social stories.

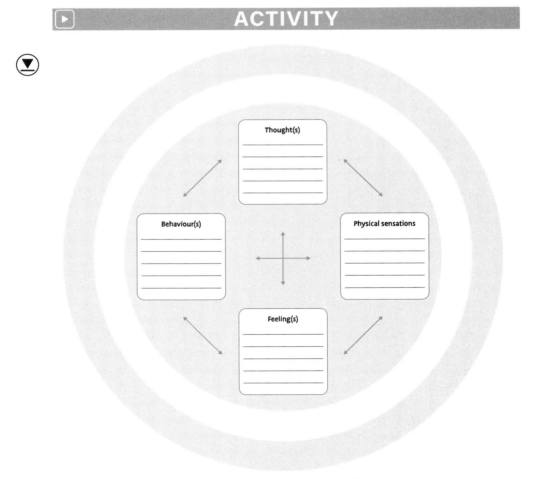

Figure 14.6: Hot cross bun and circles of influence: self-harm

SURFING THE URGE TO SELF-HARM

So far:

- You may be more aware of what urges to self-harm feel like for you.

- You may have been able to track when and where these urges tend to occur.

- You may have an idea what function certain self-harming behaviours have for you (but do not worry if you do not).

Next, we are going to going to focus on how to manage the urge to self-harm a little more. As a first step, I recommend locking away, hiding or otherwise making it more difficult to access anything that you may use to hurt yourself. This could be certain substances, or certain pieces of equipment like razor blades. This puts some distance between you and the things that you could use to hurt yourself, and makes it more likely that you will tolerate the urge a little longer than normal.

Our aim here is basically to delay the urge for as long as possible. When we do this, the urge can feel a little less intense and we can feel a little more in control. Sometimes this is called 'urge surfing'. Just like a surfer rides a wave, you can learn to 'surf out' your self-harming urges. Just like a wave will crash on the shore and disappear, so will your urge after time. This is not easy though, and takes practice! If you have been hurting yourself for a long time, then the first few times you do this you may only be able to 'surf the urge' for a matter of seconds. Over time, however, you may notice that you are able to 'surf the urge' for longer and longer. In the box on the following page is a list of activities that you could try to do when you notice a strong urge. You might not need to surf the urge for urges under 4 or 5 on your urge thermometer, so I would encourage you to practise this on the stronger urges you have that can feel more unmanageable.

When you get the urge to self-harm, try surfing the urge for as long as possible using the following strategies:

3

- Play with your pet (if you have one)
- Think of as many things as you can beginning with the letter F
- Listen to music, a podcast, the radio or an audiobook
- Write a compassionate letter to yourself (see Chapter 5, *Self-Acceptance and Self-Compassion*; I would recommend reading the self-compassion section first because self-compassion exercises can be particularly difficult for people who self-harm)
- Call a friend or helpline (the conversation does not have to be about self-harm – you could say you are struggling in general, or just have a conversation about something else!)
- Do 20 push-ups/squats (if you are able to)
- Research a period of history on the internet
- Walk around and name ten things you can see that could end up in a museum in 100 years
- Look at photos of things you like or care about
- Rip up a newspaper or magazine
- Open the fridge or freezer and feel the cold air
- Make your favourite hot or cold drink
- Do the washing/laundry
- Investigate a local folklore or myth
- Go for a walk
- Paint or draw
- Colour in (there are patterns to colour in at the end of the book)
- Write a to-do list
- Do a puzzle
- Use things from your self-soothe box (see Chapter 13, *Trauma*, for how to create one)
- Think of your safe place imagery (see Chapter 8, *Feeling Anxious*)
- Open the closest book to a random page and count all the words that begin with the letter C
- Write a short story/poem

ACTIVITY

My ideas for surfing the urge:

_____   _____

_____   _____

When you are in the moment and start to experience an urge, it can sometimes be difficult remembering all these different things you could try. It might be useful to write down exactly what you will do here, and put a bookmark or sticky note on this page, so you can flick back to it quickly.

When I get the urge to hurt myself I will do _____

I can also try _____

If that does not work I can try _____

If I have tried those things I can then do _____

If the urge is still around I can now _____

WHEN THE URGE FEELS TOO STRONG TO SURF

As I mentioned, surfing the urge is a skill that takes time. You might not be able to do it right away, but keep trying. Until then, you may find there are times when your urges feel too strong to surf. When this happens, you may need to do something that satisfies your urge, but without seriously hurting yourself. This is sometimes known as 'safer self-harm', as it often achieves the same functions of self-harm without the (potentially) serious physical consequences. What is important to remember with 'safer self-harm' is that the behaviour you are doing instead has to match what your self-harm is about. So, if you now know that pain is not important for you when you self-harm, then some of the strategies below such as snapping an elastic band on your wrist will not be as effective. Below are some suggested safer self-harm strategies to help manage the urge:

4

- Ping an elastic band or hairband on your wrist
- Squeeze ice in palm of your hand
- Clap hands together hard
- Have a cold bath/shower
- Run hands under really cold water
- Eat something really spicy or hot (e.g., a pepper, or a hot curry)
- Hit or bite a pillow or cushion
- Draw on yourself with red pen (if seeing blood is part of the reason or function for your self-harm)
- Break sticks
- Drip warm candle wax on yourself and peel off
- Squeeze a stress ball
- Scream into a pillow
- Wax your legs/armpits
- Play the drums (or get cutlery and pretend they are drumsticks!)
- Go for a run
- Rip up paper or cardboard
- Do push-ups or squats in your house

ACTIVITY

If you end up trying some of these safer self-harm strategies, it could be a good idea to write below which ones seemed to work really well for you, so you can use these again.

Safer self-harm strategies that work really well for me:

_____   _____

_____   _____

---

5   HELPLINES/WEBSITES FOR SELF-HARM

Samaritans (UK): 116 123 (open 24/7)/jo@samaritans.org

Self-injury Support (specifically for women in the UK):
0808 800 8088 or 0780 047 2908 (www.selfinjurysupport.org.uk)

YoungMinds (UK):
0808 802 5544 (parents helpline)/text YM to 85258 (https://youngminds.org.uk)

*There are more resources, both self-harm specific and more generic,
listed at the end of this book.*

CREATING A 'MANAGING MY SELF-HARM' PLAN

I hope that in this section you have been able to explore your urges a little more, and have some ideas as to how you could manage these. Next, we are going to pull this information together into a 'managing my self-harm' plan. The idea of this plan is that you have a resource that you can consult when things may be difficult for you, and urges may be escalating.

Table 14.3 is an example. You will see that I have numbered various parts of the plan. Remember at the start of this section when I said to ignore the numbers for now? Well, the information that may be useful to include in your management plan can be found in the corresponding numbered activities above. Of course, this plan is supposed to be unique to you. So if you can think of other things to go in there, then please include them. My ideas are just for guidance, or to help you if you are struggling to think. There is a blank plan after my example, which you can write in and complete yourself.

Table 14.3: Self-harm management plan: example

	Urge intensity	I will have thoughts such as	I will feel / I will feel the urge to	I will do things like / I can surf the urge by	To make myself feel good again/to distract myself I can / Others can distract me by	As a last resort, safer self-harm strategies could be
Mild urges	2	'I can feel lots of things inside but I can manage'	A bit restless / Like feelings are ever so slightly bubbling	Focus on my work / Decide I will not engage with the urge	Put on my favourite TV show / Write in my journal	
Moderate urges	5	"Things are feeling quite overwhelming"	Hit my head on the wall / Drink lots of alcohol	Naming 20 things beginning with P / Going for a walk	Coming for a walk with me / Playing video games with me	Hit my head into a pillow / Drink lots of lemonade
Strong urges	9	'I cannot cope with this'	Cut myself	Calling a helpline / Running fast on the spot	Talking to me about what you have done during the day	Squeeze ice cubes until it hurts / Use elastic bands on my wrists

Helplines I can call:
Self-injury Support: 0808 800 8088
Samaritans: 116 123

People/things that can help me in the moment:
My self-soothe box
My flat mate

Key information others need to know (e.g., medications I take, allergies I have):
None

Blank self-harm management plan

	Urge intensity	I will have thoughts such as	I will feel	I will do things like	To make myself feel good again/to distract myself I can	
Mild urges						
Moderate urges	Urge intensity	I will have thoughts such as	I will feel the urge to	I can surf the urge by	Others can distract me by	As a last resort, safer self-harm strategies could be
Strong urges	Urge intensity	I will have thoughts such as	I will feel the urge to	I can surf the urge by	Others can distract me by	As a last resort, safer self-harm strategies could be

Helplines I can call:	People/things that can help me in the moment:	Key information others need to know (e.g., medications I take, allergies I have):

IF YOU HAVE HURT YOURSELF

If you have ended up self-harming, first, do not be too hard on yourself (easier said than done, I know). I do not doubt that you have tried your best, and that on this occasion things just got too much. If your wounds or injuries are minor, it is probably good to tend to them using clean medical equipment. It is probably also a good idea to seek medical support as soon as is practical to check this over. If your wounds or injuries are not minor, seek medical support immediately. You can do this by attending your local emergency department, or by calling 999 (UK), 112 (Europe) or 911 (USA). One final thing that may help is to tell someone what has happened. This can be really difficult if other people have reacted unhelpfully to your self-harm. However, if there is someone who has responded kindly and whom you trust, then telling them what has happened may help as they can assist in getting you the support you need. Even if you do not want to tell anyone, some people find it useful to give voice to this experience by writing about it in their journal or diary.

I would also encourage you to perhaps go back to the self-harming urge diary and explore what led to this behaviour. By doing this, you may notice certain triggers that you can be more aware of next time. When you are more aware of triggers, you can try surfing the urge and distracting yourself, or using safer self-harm strategies. As I said right at the start of this chapter, you are probably not going to be able to just stop self-harming, so this is going to take time, patience and practice. It might be good to read some of the self-compassion stuff in Chapter 5, *Self-Acceptance and Self-Compassion*, so you can practise being kind to yourself if things have not gone to plan, or they are are going more slowly than you had hoped.

DOING SOMETHING ABOUT EXTERNAL TRIGGERS

In your self-harming urge diary, you may have noticed that certain people, places, things or activities seem to accompany your urge, or are there just before it starts. As you will know, a running theme in this book is the fact that the world around us can influence our mental health and wellbeing. There are ways to manage the urge to self-harm when it creeps in, but an even better way of helping is to remove or distance ourselves from external factors that trigger this urge.

The first thing to do here is to take a look at your urge diary, and look in the column labelled *Where was I? What time was it? Who was I with?* and *What was going on just before I got the urge?* This is where you may have noted any people, places or things that seemed to come before the urge. Next, notice if there are any patterns. Do stronger urges tend to always happen when you are in a particular place, or with a particular person/group? If so, there could be something important going on here. Maybe without you even being aware of it, these places or people are having a negative impact on your wellbeing. Perhaps something bad happened, or difficult memories are being brought up. Maybe these people are actually quite negative and discriminatory towards you and you have always brushed this off or ignored it. Or maybe you have noticed that the urge to self-harm always seems to arrive when you are on the internet looking at certain websites. Maybe you thought these sites were helpful, but actually they seem to be triggering for you. If you completed the hot cross bun and circles of influence as well (or instead) then you may have also captured some of these external factors there.

The final thing to do is to ask yourself, 'What is within my power to do something about this?' Options may include:

- Stopping involvement with these people, or only communicating with them when you really need to (if you have to be involved with them).

- Distancing yourself from the places that are not good for your wellbeing, or limiting your time within them (if you need to be or go there).

- Letting others know that something within an environment is not helpful for you, and seeing if this can be changed.

- If you are hearing or listening to something that you know to be unhelpful for you (and others) then you may feel able to speak up and say something.

Removing yourself or others is likely to be the best preventative thing for your urges. If it does not feel as if you can actively do anything to change the people or places around you, then at least you know that there are some ways you can manage what follows by surfing the urge. Having to do this and not feeling as if you are in control of a situation can be really tough. There is a way to retain some power and control (even if we feel as if we are not) by choosing to accept the situation we find ourselves in. This can have a strangely calming effect on us, knowing that we are *choosing* to accept our circumstances. Practising acceptance is another skill that takes time to fully master. You can find more details on how to practise acceptance in Chapter 10, *Sleep Difficulties*.

SKILLS FROM OTHER SECTIONS THAT MAY BE USEFUL FOR YOU

- Self-compassion skills from Chapter 5, *Self-Acceptance and Self-Compassion*

- Resetting fight or flight from Chapter 8, *Feeling Anxious*

- Acceptance from Chapter 10, *Sleep Difficulties*

- Self-soothe box from Chapter 13, *Trauma*

SUMMARY

- Self-harming behaviours can encompass a wide range of things, including purposefully hurting yourself with objects, restricting what you eat, binge eating or engaging in risky behaviours.

- Self-harm can have lots of different functions, and often begins as a coping strategy, though over time can become part of the problem.

- There are ways that you can 'surf the urge' to self-harm, by doing something to distract yourself until the urge begins to reduce in intensity.

- You can create a 'managing my self-harm' plan that includes what mild, moderate and strong urges feel like, and how you can surf these urges.

- Sometimes a good way of managing self-harm is to remove or distance yourself from people, places or things that could be triggers.

Space for your own thoughts, reflections, ideas, action plans

— Chapter 15 —

SUICIDE

Suicide has largely been a taboo topic. Social stories have existed, and can still exist, that if someone takes their own life, they are 'taking the cowardly way out'. This could not be further from the truth, and this harmful narrative can increase feelings of shame for the person in distress, and make it really difficult for them to talk to anyone about how they are feeling. Having suicidal thoughts is actually a fairly common experience (around one in five of the general population experience these; Casey *et al.*, 2008), and can occur for a whole range of reasons. This experience can also be thought of as occurring on a spectrum, from people having fleeting suicidal thoughts that come and go, to those who have thoughts that are always there. Suicide is not a dirty word, and is something that should be openly discussed. By not discussing suicide, we give power to the secrecy and shame that has long been associated with this intense experience of distress.

SUICIDE AND THE QUEER COMMUNITY

Rates of suicide are much higher for Queer people when compared to others (King *et al.*, 2008; Thoma *et al.*, 2019). Unique to Queer people, there are multiple things that can, at times, make life feel unmanageable. Equally, there are numerous factors that can make reaching out for help difficult. For example, asking for help can be tough because of internalized homo/bi/transphobia (e.g., 'I am not worthy of help'). Narratives that exist from others and throughout society (e.g., 'Being Queer is not natural') can also make reaching out for help difficult, as can the negative experiences Queer people may have had with healthcare professionals (e.g., invalidation, stigma). This is usually all set within a wider social story that suicide is a taboo topic that cannot be talked about, because it will 'give people ideas' (it will not) or it is just too painful to think about (it is more painful for the people living it). In fact, it is quite the opposite: talking about suicide for those who are experiencing these thoughts can actually make it less painful to manage.

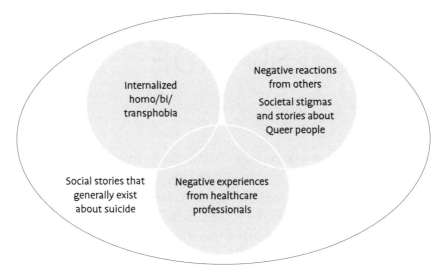

Figure 15.1: Why talking about suicide and asking for help
can be particularly tricky for Queer people

Figure 15.1 shows why talking about suicide can be really hard for Queer people, and how these challenges can overlap and interact with each other. As you can see, these specific Queer difficulties occur against the backdrop of the general social stories that exist in the world about suicide.

If you are reading this section and have had, or are having, thoughts of ending your own life, please first know that:

You are not alone.

It may not feel like it now, but you are needed in this world.

The world is a better place with you in it.

Second, please know that help is available for you. Reading this section, as you are right now, might be a really big step you have taken so far with regard to your thoughts and feelings of suicide. I hope that the following activities in this section can help you with some of the thoughts and feelings you are having at the moment. Please ignore the fact that there are some big numbers in boxes next to some of the activities. The reason for this will become apparent a little later on.

TALKING TO OTHERS

My single biggest piece of advice, which probably comes as no surprise, is that you should let someone you trust know how you are feeling. Talk to a friend, family member, colleague or healthcare professional. Alternatively, some people find it easier to talk to a stranger, and helplines such as the Samaritans can be a good option. Such people may be able to help you get support from a healthcare professional, if you are not already engaged with mental health services.

Talking to a healthcare professional is beneficial as they can provide you with personalized advice and ideas for the next steps. However, I am very aware that some Queer people have, or have had, troubled relationships with healthcare professionals. If this applies to you, first I must apologize on behalf of the healthcare professional world. No one should ever reach out for help and be made to feel belittled, invalidated or dismissed (whether this is related to mental or physical health). Because of this I am aware that it is very easy for me to write *'go and speak to a healthcare professional'* when this could be tricky for you.

There are lots of healthcare professionals out there who truly want to help you. Here are five things that may help with making your decision as to whether and who to tell:

1. If you have had a bad experience with a particular professional, ask your healthcare provider if you can speak with someone else instead.

2. Sometimes saying words out loud is too tough. Perhaps you can write down how you are feeling and email, post or hand it to a professional? That way they can call you or 'speak first', which may make things feel slightly easier.

3. Take a trusted friend/family member/colleague with you. You are perfectly within your rights to have someone with you during a consultation if you prefer this.

4. If physically going to a healthcare building is not possible, or feels too much, ask for a telephone or video consultation instead. This medium of communication is becoming more and more common within the healthcare world.

5. Be prepared that the healthcare professional may have to tell other professionals in order to get the appropriate help for you. This should

always be done in consultation with you. A lot of people are scared that they will be detained or 'sectioned' if they tell a professional they are feeling suicidal. This is rarely the case, and doing things against a person's wishes is always the last resort for a healthcare professional. Nevertheless, I totally get that this is a legitimate concern for many. If this is worrying for you, share this concern with the professional. Perhaps you can say 'I have something I want to tell you and I know that you may have to get other people involved to help me. I want all decisions, as much as possible, to be done in collaboration with me.'

Even though you may not want to tell anyone how you are feeling, why not have a go at writing who you might be able to tell if you felt able to? There may be some blank sections dependent on your personal circumstances.

▶ ACTIVITY

1

A trusted friend: _____

A trusted family member: _____

A helpline I could call: _____

A trusted healthcare professional: _____

A trusted colleague at work: _____

A trusted teacher/lecturer: _____

Others I trust: _____

Others I trust: _____

Others I trust: _____

IDENTIFYING IMPORTANT THOUGHTS, FEELINGS AND BEHAVIOURS

On the following page is a wheel that is divided up into six segments (Figure 15.2). This first wheel is about thoughts you may be having about suicide. While this is by no means an exclusive list, this wheel and the segments within it are things that we know are common in those who are thinking about suicide.

This is a self-reflective exercise and you can shade in each segment based on how strongly you feel it applies to you. Think of number 1 as meaning 'not at all', 2 as 'kind of', 3 as 'most of the time' and 4 as 'all of the time'. For example, if you have thoughts of ending your life that are there all the time, you can shade the whole of the segment in.

After you have done this, there is then space to write about any barriers to acting on these thoughts, or any reasons that you can list not to act on these thoughts. For example, using the above example again of having thoughts of ending your life that are there all the time, you may list the fact that no one would look after your pet if you did act on these thoughts. You might want to complete this part of the exercise after you have looked at the section labelled 'number 5', as that gives you more examples of things that can stop you acting on such thoughts and feelings.

This exercise is not intended as a professional suicide risk assessment. Rather, I hope that by considering each of these areas you can identify things that you may need help or support with. I would suggest anything that you have shaded in as a 3 or 4 suggests that you might need support with this, though of course you may have shaded something in as a 1 or 2 and would like support with this too. If you do shade in many 3s or 4s, try not to panic and think that things are hopeless. Likewise, if you have only shaded in 1s or 2s, this does not diminish or invalidate any suffering you are currently experiencing. Help and support is available in this chapter.

ACTIVITY

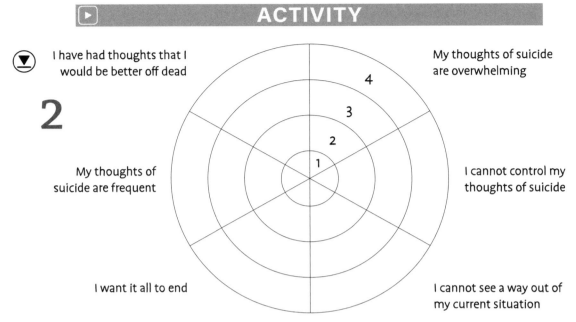

Figure 15.2: Suicide prevention wheel: thoughts

What stops me from acting on any of these thoughts:

_____

_____

_____

_____

_____

_____

_____

This second wheel is about any suicidal feelings you may have. Again, this is not an exclusive list. As before, shade in each segment as you think it applies to you and your experience. After this, there is space for you to list anything that stops you acting on these feelings. There are no right or wrong answers for listing things that prevent you from doing this – if it stops you from acting on such feelings then it is worth writing it down.

ACTIVITY

3

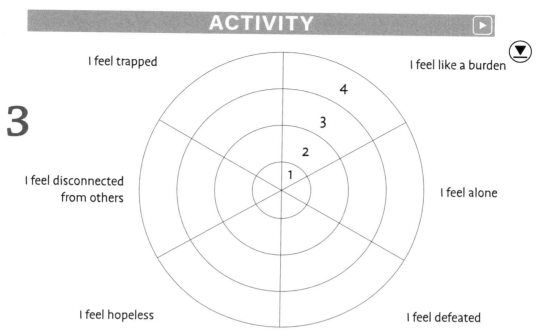

Figure 15.3: Suicide prevention wheel: feelings

What stops me from acting on any of these feelings:

_____

_____

_____

_____

_____

_____

_____

This final wheel lists any behaviours or things you may be doing/have done. Same as before, if you want to do this exercise then shade in each segment as it applies to you. Afterwards, you can list anything that stops you going through with these behaviours, or that makes such behaviours less damaging or life-threatening.

4

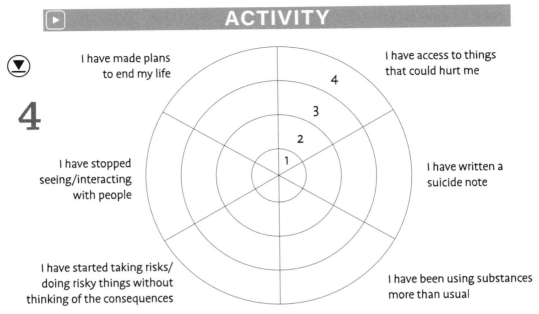

Figure 15.4: Suicide prevention wheel: behaviours

What stops me from acting on any of these behaviours:

_____

_____

_____

_____

_____

_____

_____

First, well done on completing the above exercises if you did – it takes courage to look at areas of your life that are difficult or distressing. If you did not, then well done on recognizing that now may not be the right time to do so. Reading this as you are might be enough for you to begin thinking about the next steps.

WHAT STOPS YOU FROM ENDING YOUR LIFE?

This next exercise could be difficult for some people. If you are feeling low, it can be tricky to think about good things in your life, or reasons to stay alive. However distressing things may be, you are at least reading this, which suggests to me that there is a small part of you that wants to explore alternatives to suicide.

Try to list three things that would stop you from ending your life, or would make you seriously reconsider going through with any plans that you may have made. This can be anything – ranging from a pet you have, to family/friends/colleagues you like spending time with, to missing your favourite Netflix show. Something that might be stopping you is ambivalence – perhaps you are just not sure if you want to live or die. Any reasons that make you pause and think about staying alive can be jotted down on the following page, and I have given a list of possible reasons for you to consider in the box to the right too. It is OK if you cannot think of three. If you can think of more then please jot these down too. You might have started to do this when thinking about any important thoughts, feelings or behaviours from the above exercise, which you can list here too. Otherwise, you might have waited until this section before filling out those boxes if you were not sure what to include. I have included some examples for you to think about, though of course please list any that are relevant for your own individual circumstance.

▶ ACTIVITY

_____ would stop

me from ending my life because

_____

_____

_____

_____ would stop

me from ending my life because

_____

_____

_____

_____ would stop

me from ending my life because

_____

_____

_____

5

Job I have to go to

University course/society I attend

Favourite food/drink I would miss

Family/friends/colleagues I care about

Favourite TV shows I would miss

Internet forums/chatrooms I use

Video games I play

Impact this may have on family/friends

Ambivalence – not sure if I want to die

Religion/faith/belief system

Festival/music event I would miss

Could not do Queer activism

Country/city I want to visit

_____

I really want to do _____

I do not want to leave my pet

No one would look after

_____

I really value _____

I do not want others to be impacted

THINGS YOU CAN DO WHEN THOUGHTS AND FEELINGS GET TOO MUCH

A famous suicide researcher called Edwin Schneidman once said, 'Never kill yourself when you are suicidal.' The thoughts and feelings that come with this experience are very rarely constant, and periods of suicidal feelings *do not last forever*. When these thoughts and feelings are really strong, things can seem much, much darker than they might be. If you can engage with your thoughts and feelings in a slightly different way when you feel like this, this might be enough to ride out some of the most painful parts of that experience.

Below are three boxes with strategies, tips and ideas that you could do when any of those segments in the wheels above are feeling really strong for you. There is space within the box for you to write some of your own suggestions too, if you have some:

Thoughts

6

- Think of my thoughts as leaves passing by on a stream – they are there, I can see them, and I am choosing to let them float past
- Write my thoughts down on a piece of paper and screw them up and put in the bin
- Distract from thoughts by watching my favourite movie, listening to music or calling a friend
- Tell myself 'these thoughts will not last forever'
- Distract myself by going to my self-soothe box (see Chapter 13, *Trauma*) and using some of these items
- Go for a brisk walk

_____   _____

_____   _____

Feelings

7

- Tell myself that my feelings are not facts, and although how I feel is valid and real, I should not read too much into them
- If I am feeling disconnected from others, I could call a friend or helpline and talk to someone, or use an internet chat forum
- Tell myself that 'these feelings will not last forever'
- If I am feeling hopeless, I could remind myself that I am reading this book and therefore a part of me wants things to be different
- If I am feeling defeated, I can tell myself that the sun will rise again tomorrow, bringing hope for things to be different

_____   _____

_____   _____

Behaviours

8

- If I am or have been using more substances, I could reduce my access to these, for example by handing over excess alcohol or drugs to a friend
- If I have access to things that I could use to hurt myself, I could hand these to someone if possible (I can also hand pills into a pharmacy/doctor). If I cannot hand them to someone, I could at least lock them away. If things are locked away at least this minimizes the chance of any impulsive behaviour
- If I have stopped seeing people, I could act opposite to this and make a plan to see someone for a coffee, or speak to them on the phone/video chat, or I could connect to a local Queer group

_____   _____

_____   _____

9

HELPLINES WHEN FEELING SUICIDAL

Samaritans (UK): 116 123 (open 24/7)/jo@samaritans.org

Papyrus (UK) 0800 068 41 41 (open 9am–midnight every day)/pat@papyrus.uk.org

CALM (UK): 0800 58 58 58 (open 5pm–midnight every day)

National Suicide Prevention Lifeline (USA): 800 273 TALK (800 273 8255)

TrevorLifeline (USA) 866 488 7386 (open 24/7)/text START to 678678

American Foundation for Suicide Prevention (USA):
800 273 8255/text TALK to 741741

There are more resources, both suicide specific and more generic, available at the end of this book.

CREATING A SAFETY PLAN

So far, with the activities that you may have completed, you might have an idea of some things that you could do if you are feeling suicidal. We are now going to use these to create a 'safety plan'. This is a plan that helps you think of alternative things you can do when you are feeling suicidal, including how you can spot that things are becoming more difficult for you. The key thing with a safety plan is to _have this ready in advance_. It is really, really hard to do any planning when you are distressed or experiencing intense suicidal thoughts or feelings. If you can plan in advance for what to do when you feel like that, this will massively help.

On the following page is an example safety plan. You will see that I have numbered each part of the plan. Remember at the start of this section when I said to ignore the numbers for now? Well, the information that may be useful to include in your safety plan can be found in the corresponding numbered activities above. Of course, this safety plan is unique to you. So, if you can think of other things to go in there, then please include them. My ideas are just for guidance, or to help you if you are struggling to think. There is a blank safety plan after my example that you can write in yourself.

Table 15.1: Suicide safety plan example

When things are good	I will have thoughts such as *'Life is good today'* 2	I will feel *Quite happy* *Like I matter* 3	I will do things like *Watch TV* *Chat to friends on the phone* 4	Others will know that I am OK because *I will answer the phone when they call*	To keeps things going well I will *Stay in touch with others* *Manage my anxiety* 6, 7, 8	To keep things going well other people can help me by *Checking in with me if I am anxious*
When things are rocky	I will have thoughts such as *'Nobody really cares about me'*	I will feel *Sad* *Hopeless* *Like a burden*	I will do things like *Withdraw to my room* *Not talk to friends*	Others will know things are rocky because *I will not log into Facebook much* *I will just say I am fine*	To help make things better I could *Eat my favourite foods*	Other people can help me by *Calling me – I find it easier to answer calls than making them*
When things are bad	I will have thoughts such as *'I do not want to be alive anymore'*	I will feel *Like I do not matter* *Intense sadness*	I will do things like *Make a plan to end my life*	Others will know things are bad because *I will not answer my phone*	To help make things better I could *Tell myself these thoughts and feelings will pass*	Other people can help me by *Coming round to my house*
When I am in immediate need of help	I will have thoughts such as *'I want to die right now'*	I will feel *Like I do not belong* *Totally hopeless*	I will do things like *Drink too much alcohol*	Others will know I need immediate help because *I do not answer my phone*	To stop me making an attempt on my life I will *Throw away my alcohol* *Call Samaritans*	Other people can help me by *Coming round to my house and sitting with me, even if I do not feel worthy*

9

Helplines I can call:

Samaritans – 116 123

In an emergency 999/911

1, 6

People/things that can help me in the moment:

Hug my pet dog

Listen to music so voices go away

Act opposite to loneliness by calling someone

5

Reasons for staying alive:

No one would look after my dog

I would not be able to volunteer at the youth group

Key information others need to know (e.g., medications I take, allergies I have):

Allergic to penicillin

Take antidepressant medication twice a day

Blank suicide safety plan

	I will have thoughts such as	I will feel	I will do things like	Others will know that I am OK because	To keeps things going well I will	To keep things going well other people can help me by
When things are good						
When things are rocky	I will have thoughts such as	I will feel	I will do things like	Others will know things are rocky because	To help make things better I could	Other people can help me by

When things are bad	I will have thoughts such as	I will feel	I will do things like	Others will know things are bad because	To help make things better I could	Other people can help me by
When I am in immediate need of help	I will have thoughts such as	I will feel	I will do things like	Others will know I need immediate help because	To stop me making an attempt on my life I will	Other people can help me by

Helplines I can call:	People/things that can help me in the moment:	Reasons for staying alive:	Key information others need to know (e.g., medications I take, allergies I have):

At the start of this chapter (box numbered 1), I asked you to think about some people that you might be able to speak to about your suicidal thoughts. Now you have completed your suicide safety plan, I wonder if you could share this plan with any of them? Or, maybe you have thought of someone else not on your original list whom you could share this plan with? If you want to, you can write their names below. You can, of course, share your safety plan with as many trusted people as you like. This is because sometimes things can feel so dark and lonely that our ability to think properly becomes foggy. If someone else knows the 'signs' to look out for in you that let them know things are becoming difficult, they can perhaps step in to help.

I could share my safety plan with _____

I could share my safety plan with _____

I could share my safety plan with _____

PREVENTING SUICIDE: CONSIDERING EXTERNAL FACTORS

Now that you have created your safety plan, it is also worth considering if there are any external factors, or things in your environment, that could be contributing to your suicidal thoughts and feelings. On the following page is a fourth wheel, with things that could be linked to how you are currently feeling. As before, you can shade in each segment to see how relevant this is for you. As before, think of number 1 as meaning 'not at all', number 2 is 'kind of', number 3 is 'most of the time' and number 4 is 'all of the time'. For example, if you engage with social media all the time and it is not doing anything for your mental health or wellbeing, you can shade the whole of the segment in.

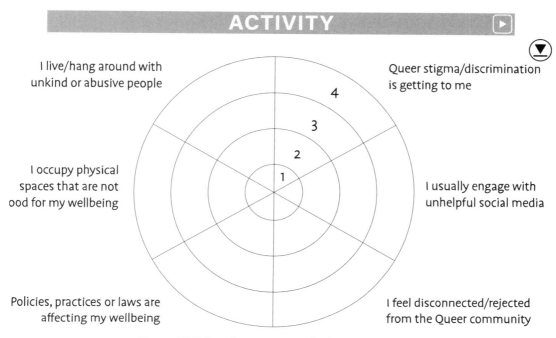

I live/hang around with unkind or abusive people

Queer stigma/discrimination is getting to me

I occupy physical spaces that are not ood for my wellbeing

I usually engage with unhelpful social media

Policies, practices or laws are affecting my wellbeing

I feel disconnected/rejected from the Queer community

Figure 15.5: Suicide prevention wheel: external factors

If you have shaded in any of these six segments as a '3' or '4', I would suggest that these require some attention. Of course, you may have shaded something in as a '1' or a '2', and still want to think about this. Below, I will briefly highlight how you can make changes in each of these areas.

PREVENTING SUICIDE: BUILDING CONNECTION

We know that loneliness, disconnection from others and feeling like you do not belong can be risks for suicide. These things can be really prevalent for Queer people. Building connection to other people, or other things, is a great way to counter this. You could do this by searching online for local Queer groups, local interest groups or local sports/hobby clubs that you could join. If you are at university, there will be lots of societies that you can join. You could also build connection online by starting a blog that other people can engage with, or by joining in with online discussion groups. You could also volunteer for a local charity, or befriender service. Religion can also be a great way for people to feel connected to other people of faith, and/or to a higher power. As mentioned in Chapter 13, *Trauma*, be sure to engage with religion or belief systems that support you.

PREVENTING SUICIDE: WHAT YOU CAN DO ABOUT QUEER DISCRIMINATION

Being discriminated against because of who you are is not OK, and I am sorry if you have experienced this. I would first encourage you to report this to the police if you feel able to. Second, sharing your experiences with a close friend or family member may help, rather than keeping it all to yourself. Third, if you can, I would encourage you to distance yourself from individuals who may directly discriminate against you. See the section below for ideas for how to do this.

If you are experiencing Queer discrimination or stigma through other mediums, such as the media or TV/film, see if you can switch off and disengage from this for a while to take care of your own mental health and wellbeing. If you wanted to, you could send a complaint to the TV/film producers or media agency expressing your feelings about discrimination, prejudice or stigma, and you could suggest ways that they could do things differently.

PREVENTING SUICIDE: WHEN POLICIES, PRACTICES OR LAWS AFFECT YOU

Sometimes policies that you must adhere to as part of your job, or laws that exist in your country, can negatively impact on your wellbeing, which could in turn relate to suicidal thoughts and feelings. If this is happening, I encourage you to write to, email or call people in positions of power who can change these. If this relates to policies or procedures at work, you could speak to a trusted manager or to your human resources department. If it is a law affecting your wellbeing, you could join (or set up) a campaign to change this. This could include signing (or starting) a petition to government. This may be more difficult in countries that have active anti-Queer laws. If you think your life is in danger from the government because of your Queer identity, you can always seek asylum in the closest 'safe' country. This would involve a huge change; however, I think it is worth spelling this out for anyone who is not aware that this is an option.

One other thing you could do would be to run as an elected individual in your local, regional or national government, healthcare sectors or educational establishments. This might sound like a massive thing, but there is a broad range of positions that people can be elected to, including school governor positions, local neighbourhood officers/councillors and community representatives. By doing this you could have some direct influence over policies, practices and laws. Not only could this be beneficial for you, but it could also help improve the wellbeing of many other Queer people. It is important to realize just how powerful Queer visibility can be as a suicide prevention strategy in itself. For other people, seeing a Queer person in an influential position can fill them with hope, positivity and help them feel as if their existence is valid and worthy.

PREVENTING SUICIDE: DISTANCING YOURSELF FROM TOXIC PEOPLE

There may be people in your life who belittle you, put you down or make you feel worthless. Even if these people are your birth family, you do not have to put up with toxic people in your life who bring you down. To distance yourself from these people, try talking to them and expressing how they are making you feel. It is best to do this in a neutral space, such as a coffee shop or park – a place where you can feel in control, and you can leave if you need/want to. If speaking face to face feels too much, you could send them an email, message on social media or even write them a letter. If you do not get a reply, or do not get a constructive or apologetic message back, you know that you have at least expressed what you think and can walk away feeling in control of the situation. If you have toxic people on social media, then block them if you need to.

PREVENTING SUICIDE: DISTANCING YOURSELF FROM TOXIC ENVIRONMENTS

Sometimes people keep going to places that are not actually positive or helpful for their wellbeing. An example of this could be a Queer nightclub. This environment could have started as a place of liberation, expression and fun for someone. However, this may also be a place where someone had a negative experience (e.g., an argument with close friends) or even traumatic experience (e.g., sexual assault in the toilets). Going to this particular environment may be a routine that this person has got into, without realizing that every time they go to this nightclub they feel anxious, low in mood, experience trauma symptoms or feel bad about themselves. These things could ultimately lead to suicidal thoughts and feelings. Recognizing environments or places that are not good for our mental health and wellbeing helps to ensure that we can distance ourselves from them.

PREVENTING SUICIDE: CHANGING YOUR RELATIONSHIP WITH SOCIAL MEDIA

DID YOU KNOW?

Suicide in the UK used to be illegal. Because of this, it was technically an offence to take your own life. This is why the term 'commit' suicide was coined and used. Now, we tend to say 'die by suicide', as this carries less of the historic stigma.

Impact on mental health

Because suicide was an offence, people internalized a sense that this was a shameful behaviour that must not be spoken about. People who felt suicidal usually did not tell anyone about their distress, which often led to feeling extremely isolated and disconnected from loved ones. Over time, people did not talk about suicide because it had huge moral, religious and legal implications. The historic connotations of suicide being illegal are perhaps one reason why this is still such a difficult topic to talk about today.

Social media can be a force for good, or a force for bad. On social media, we can get caught up in a cycle of seeking validation from 'likes' to the point that if someone does not like a post or picture we put up, we can begin to think negatively about ourselves. To counter this, it may be a good idea to try a social media detox. Log out of any social media apps for a few days, and concentrate on doing things that are good for your wellbeing.

As well as this, there may be some people on social media who make us feel bad about ourselves. This could be because they say horrible things, but it could be because they seem to have the 'perfect' life. People will always present the absolute best version of themselves on social media, and this is not representative of how they will be living their life all the time. If this comparison between their life and yours is making you feel bad about yourself, unfollow them or block them. You need to do what you need to do, to protect your own wellbeing.

PREVENTING SUICIDE: HELPING SOMEONE WHO IS SUICIDAL

One of your friends, family members or fellow students/colleagues may tell you that they are feeling suicidal. This can be a really difficult thing to hear, whether you expect it or not, and it has also probably taken lots of strength and courage for the individual to tell someone they trust. You could very well be on someone's list of people whom they trust and wanted to share their thoughts and feelings with.

Here are five basic tips I have for responding when someone tells you they are having suicidal thoughts/feelings, in order to keep them **ALIVE**:

- **Acknowledge:** Acknowledge that you have heard that they are in distress.

- **Listen:** Sometimes it is not helpful to jump straight into problem-solving mode. Often what people need at the time is someone to just listen to what they have to say in a non-judgemental and empathic way.

- **Invite others in:** Unless you are a trained professional, the chances are you are not going to have tons of knowledge about suicide prevention and assessing suicide risk. For this reason, it is important that other people are invited into the conversation. This does not have to be a healthcare professional right away; perhaps it can be another trusted person. It can be really difficult if the person who has told you about their thoughts has asked you not to tell anyone else. It is really important that you check out why they do not want to tell anyone else, and if there are things you can do together to make it easier to tell others.

- **Validate:** Someone is telling you something really personal and upsetting. It is OK for you to validate how they are feeling. You can do so non-verbally, by showing them you are listening and engaged in the conversation (maintaining gaze, open posture). You can also validate what someone is saying verbally, for example by saying, 'That sounds really difficult' or, 'I am here to listen' or, 'How can I help?'

- **Explore options together:** Together with the person, you can explore what options they have available. Can they call a suicide helpline? Can they create a safety plan? Can they book an appointment with their doctor? Can they go to the emergency department?

The SHOUT service in the UK provides support and can debrief people who have supported someone who has been suicidal, as well as supporting the suicidal person themselves. You can text SHOUT to 85258.

IF YOU HAVE BEEN BEREAVED BY SUICIDE

If someone close to you has died by suicide, this can be incredibly tough to manage by yourself. You may be feeling a mix of emotions, and it is totally normal for your emotions to fluctuate day to day, or even hour to hour. Taking care of yourself is really important, and activities from Chapter 5, *Self-Acceptance and Self-Compassion*, could be useful for you to look at. There are also specialist organizations that you can contact, and some are listed at the end of this book.

SKILLS FROM OTHER SECTIONS THAT MAY BE USEFUL FOR YOU

- Self-compassion skills from Chapter 5, *Self-Acceptance and Self-Compassion*

- Resetting fight or flight from Chapter 8, *Feeling Anxious*

- Behavioural activation from Chapter 9, *Feeling Low*

- Self-soothe box from Chapter 13, *Trauma*

SUMMARY

- Talking about suicide can be really difficult, though having suicidal thoughts and feelings is a common experience for lots of Queer people.

- Talking to people you trust about your suicidal thoughts is really important.

- You can create a suicide safety plan, including what you can do for yourself when things get difficult, and what others can do to support you.

- Thinking about things in your life that could be contributing to suicidal thoughts and feelings is equally as important, and there are ways to change these.

- Someone you know may tell you about suicidal thoughts or feelings they are having, and it is good to know how to respond to this.

Space for your own thoughts, reflections, ideas, action plans

— Chapter 16 —

KEEPING WELL PLAN

Below is a blank 'keeping well' worksheet. You can use this worksheet to create a personalized plan that works for you, for whatever wellbeing goal you are working towards, or whatever mental health difficulty (or difficulties) you are experiencing. It might be helpful for you to go back through this book and identify any particular strategies, skills or activities that you liked, and list them all in one place here.

General hopes/goals for the future:	Specific goal I want to work on/ achieve, or a specific difficulty I want to think about:

What I can do personally to keep myself well:	What I can change/influence in the environment to keep myself well:

What others can do in my social network to assist me in keeping well:	What support organizations and resources I could access if needed:

If I am in immediate need of support, I could call:	If I am in immediate need of support, I could try doing:

Resources

AKT (England only): www.akt.org.uk, gethelp@akt.org.uk

Association for Cognitive Analytic Therapy (ACAT; UK): www.acat.me.uk

Deaf Rainbow UK, provides information, represents and supports deaf people who are either embracing their true selves and/or identify as LGBTQIA: http://deaflgbtiqa.org.uk

Equality Network, an organization for LGBTI people in Scotland: www.equality-network.org

Galop (UK): 020 7704 2040, HateCrime@galop.org.uk (LGBT+ hate crime helpline); 0800 999 5428, help@galop.org.uk (LGBT+ domestic abuse helpline)

Gay and Lesbian Alliance Against Defamation (GLAAD) (USA): www.glaad.org

George House Trust (HIV-specific; UK): 0161 274 4499, talk@ght.org.uk

Guided meditation scripts: www.mindfulnessexercises.com/free-guided-meditation-scripts

Human Rights Campaign (USA & Canada): www.hrc.org

LGBT Foundation (UK): 0345 330 3030, info@lgbt.foundation

LGBT National Help Center (USA): 888 843 4566 4564 (national hotline); 800 246 7743 (youth talkline); 888 234 7243 (senior hotline)

Mermaids (young trans, non-binary and gender diverse people; UK): 0808 801 0400 (Monday–Friday, 9am–9pm), info@mermaidsuk.org.uk

Mypronouns: www.mypronouns.org

National Autistic Society (stories from LGBTQI people with a diagnosis of autism): www.autism.org.uk/advice-and-guidance/stories/celebrating-pride-month-tom-moran

Parents and Friends of Lesbians and Gays (PFLAG; USA): www.pflag.org

Pink Therapy (UK): www.pinktherapy.com

Regard: http://regard.org.uk

SHOUT (UK): Text SHOUT to 85258 for immediate support

Stonewall (UK): www.stonewall.org.uk

Switchboard LGBT Helpline (UK): 0300 330 0630, chris@switchboard.lgbt

Terrence Higgins Trust (HIV-specific; UK): 0808 802 1221, info@tht.org.uk (Monday–Friday, 10am–6pm, Saturday and Sunday 10am–1pm)

The Proud Trust (UK): www.theproudtrust.org, info@theproudtrust.org

UK Black Pride (promotes unity, solidarity and cooperation among all LGBTQ people of African, Asian, Caribbean, Middle Eastern and Latin American descent): www.ukblackpride.org.uk

Eating difficulty specific

Anorexia & Bulimia Care (UK): 0300 011 1213, www.anorexiabulimiacare.org.uk

Beat (UK): 0808 801 0677, www.beateatingdisorders.org.uk

Duke Health (USA): https://eatingdisorders.dukehealth.org

National Centre for Eating Disorders (UK): 0845 838 2040, https://eating-disorders.org.uk

Overeaters Anonymous (UK): www.oagb.org.uk

Self-harm specific

Battle Scars (UK): www.battle-scars-self-harm.org.uk
distrACT app (free download)
International Society for Study of Self-Injury: www.itriples.org
National Health Service (UK): www.nhs.uk/conditions/self-harm

Suicide specific

Alliance of Hope (USA; online support forum): https://forum.allianceofhope.org
Cruse Bereavement (UK): 0808 808 1677, helpline@cruse.org.uk (Monday–Friday, 9–5pm; extended hours to 8pm on Tuesdays, Wednesdays and Thursdays)
Winston's Wish (UK): 0808 802 2021, ask@winstonswish.org (Monday–Friday, 9–5pm)

Mindful colouring resources

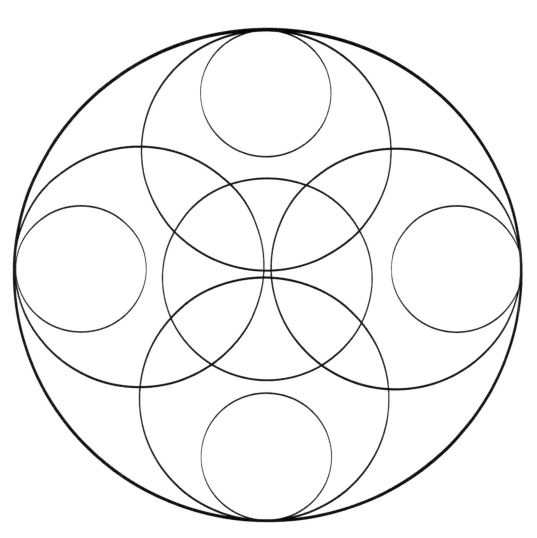

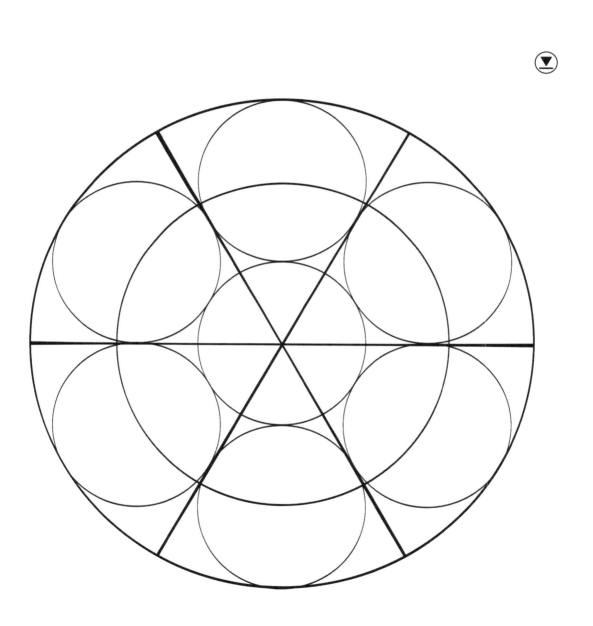

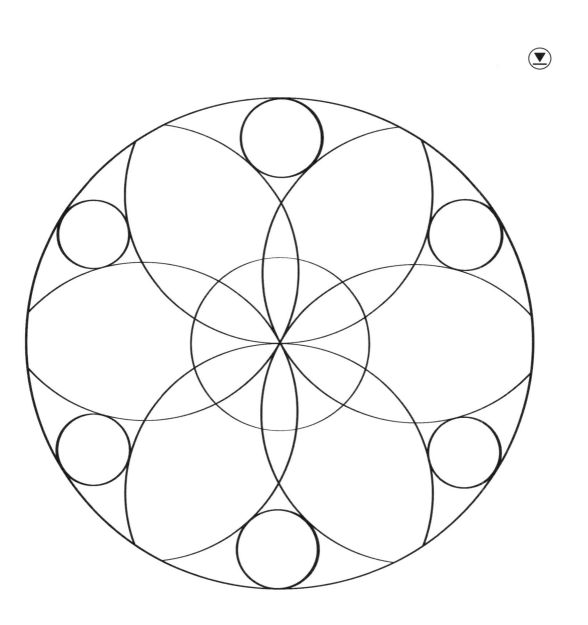

References

Introduction

Johnstone, L. & Boyle, M. *et al.* (2018). *The Power Threat Meaning Framework: Towards the identification of patterns in emotional distress, unusual experiences and troubled or troubling behaviour, as an alternative to functional psychiatric diagnosis*. Leicester: British Psychological Society. www.bps.org.uk/PTM-Main.

Glossary

Beck, J.S. (1964). *Cognitive Therapy: Basics and Beyond*. New York, NY: Guilford Press.

de Shazer, S. (1985). *Keys to Solution in Brief Therapy*. New York, NY: W.W. Norton.

Gilbert, P. (2010). *Compassion Focused Therapy: The CBT Distinctive Features Series*. New York, NY: Routledge.

Hayes, S.C., Strosahl, K.D. & Wilson, K.G. (2012). *Acceptance and Commitment Therapy: The Process and Practice of Mindful Change* (second edition). New York, NY: Guilford Press.

Johnstone, L. & Boyle, M. *et al.* (2018). *The Power Threat Meaning Framework: Towards the identification of patterns in emotional distress, unusual experiences and troubled or troubling behaviour, as an alternative to functional psychiatric diagnosis*. Leicester: British Psychological Society. www.bps.org.uk/PTM-Main.

Kabat-Zinn J. (1982). 'An outpatient program in behavioral medicine for chronic pain patients based on the practice of mindfulness meditation: Theoretical considerations and preliminary results.' *General Hospital Psychiatry, 4*(1), 33–47. https://doi.org/10.1016/0163-8343(82)90026-3.

Kabat-Zinn, J. (1990). *Full Catastrophe Living: Using the Wisdom of your Body and Mind to Face Stress, Pain, and Illness*. New York, NY: Dell Publishing.

Linehan, M.M. (1993). *Diagnosis and Treatment of Mental Disorders. Cognitive-Behavioral Treatment of Borderline Personality Disorder*. New York, NY: Guilford Press.

Ryle, A. (1995). *Cognitive Analytic Therapy: Developments in Theory and Practice*. Chichester: John Wiley & Sons.

Selvini-Palazzoli, M., Boscolo, L., Cecchin, G. & Prata, G. (1978). *Paradox and Counterparadox: A New Model in the Therapy of the Family in Schizophrenic Transaction* (translator, E.V. Burt). Lanham, MD: Jason Aronson.

Selvini-Palazzoli, M., Boscolo, L., Cecchin, G. & Prata, G. (1980). 'Hypothesizing-circularity-neutrality: Three guidelines for the conductor of the session.' *Family Process, 19*, 3–12.

White, M. & Epston, D. (1990). *Narrative Means to Therapeutic Ends*. New York, NY: W.W. Norton.

Queer Mental Health: The Basics

Beck, J.S. (1964) *Cognitive Therapy: Basics and Beyond*. New York, NY: Guilford Press.

Bronfenbrenner, U. (1977). 'Toward an experimental ecology of human development.' *American Psychologist, 32*(7), 513–531. https://doi.org/10.1037/0003-066X.32.7.513.

Meyer, I.H. (2003). 'Prejudice, social stress, and mental health in lesbian, gay, and bisexual populations: conceptual issues and research evidence.' *Psychological Bulletin, 129*(5), 674–697. https://doi.org/10.1037/0033-2909.129.5.674.

Padesky, C.A. & Mooney, K.A. (1990). 'Presenting the cognitive model to clients.' *International Cognitive Therapy Newsletter, 6*, 13–14. www.padesky.com.

Self-Acceptance and Self-Compassion

Irons, C. & Beaumont, E. (2017). *The Compassionate Mind Workbook*. London: Robinson.

Linehan, M.M. (1993). *Diagnosis and Treatment of Mental Disorders. Cognitive-Behavioral Treatment of Borderline Personality Disorder*. New York, NY: Guilford Press.

Queer Relationships

Linehan, M.M. (1993). *Diagnosis and Treatment of Mental Disorders. Cognitive-Behavioral Treatment of Borderline Personality Disorder*. New York, NY: Guilford Press.

Linehan, M.M. (2015). *DBT® Skills Training Manual* (second edition). New York, NY: Guilford Press.

Maupin, A. (2017). *Logical Family: A Memoir*. London: Penguin.

Pink Therapy (2021). What does GSRD mean? Retrieved from: www.linkedin.com/pulse/what-does-gsrd-mean-dominic-davies.

Rathus, J.H. & Miller, A.L. (2015). *DBT® Skills Manual for Adolescents*. New York, NY: Guilford Press.

Intersectionality and Me

Crenshaw, K. (1989). 'Demarginalizing the Intersection of Race and Sex: A Black Feminist Critique of Antidiscrimination Doctrine, Feminist Theory and Antiracist Politics.' University of Chicago Legal Forum: Article 8.

Equality Act (2010). Retrieved from: www.legislation.gov.uk/ukpga/2010/15/contents.

Equality Network (2016). Retrieved from: www.youtube.com/watch?v=yqTCAuj78ac.

Lorde, A. (1984). *Sister Outsider – Essays and Speeches*. Berkeley, CA: Crossing Press.

Feeling Anxious

King, M., Semlyen, J., Tai, S.S., Killaspy, H. *et al.* (2008). 'A systematic review of mental disorder, suicide, and deliberate self harm in lesbian, gay and bisexual people.' *BMC Psychiatry, 8*, 70. https://doi.org/10.1186/1471-244X-8-70.

Valentine, S.E. & Shipherd, J.C. (2018). 'A systematic review of social stress and mental health among transgender and gender non-conforming people in the United States.' *Clinical Psychology Review, 66*, 24–38. https://doi.org/10.1016/j.cpr.2018.03.003.

Feeling Low

King, M., Semlyen, J., Tai, S.S., Killaspy, H. *et al.* (2008). 'A systematic review of mental disorder, suicide, and deliberate self harm in lesbian, gay and bisexual people.' *BMC Psychiatry, 8*, 70. https://doi.org/10.1186/1471-244X-8-70.

Valentine, S.E. & Shipherd, J.C. (2018). 'A systematic review of social stress and mental health among transgender and gender non-conforming people in the United States.' *Clinical Psychology Review, 66*, 24–38. https://doi.org/10.1016/j.cpr.2018.03.003.

Veale, D. (2008). 'Behavioural activation for depression.' *Advances in Psychiatric Treatment, 14*(1), 29–36. https://doi.org/10.1192/apt.bp.107.004051.

Eating Difficulties

Boehmer, U., Bowen, D.J. & Bauer, G.R. (2007). 'Overweight and obesity in sexual-minority women: evidence from population-based data.' *American Journal of Public Health, 97*(6), 1134–1140. https://doi.org/10.2105/AJPH.2006.088419.

Feldman, M.B. & Meyer, I.H. (2007). 'Eating disorders in diverse lesbian, gay, and bisexual populations.' *International Journal of Eating Disorders, 40*(3), 218–226. https://doi.org/10.1002/eat.20360.

Keys, A., Brozek, J., Henshel, A., Mickelson, O. & Taylor, H.L. (1950). *The Biology of Human Starvation (Vols. 1–2)*. Minneapolis, MN: University of Minnesota Press.

Parker, L.L. & Harriger, J.A. (2020). 'Eating disorders and disordered eating behaviors in the LGBT population: a review of the literature.' *International Journal of Eating Disorders, 8*, 51. https://doi.org/10.1186/s40337-020-00327-y.

Struble, C.B., Lindley, L.L., Montgomery, K., Hardin, J. & Burcin, M. (2010). 'Overweight and obesity in lesbian and bisexual college women.' *Journal of American College Health, 59*(1), 51–56. https://doi.org/10.1080/07448481.2010.483703.

Shame

Harris, R. (2008). *The Happiness Trap: How to Stop Struggling and Start Living*. Boston, MA: Trumpeter Books.

White, M. & Epston, D. (1990). *Narrative Means to Therapeutic Ends*. New York, NY: W.W. Norton.

Self-harm

Dunlop, B.J., Hartley, S., Oladokun, O. & Taylor, P. (2020). 'Bisexuality and Non-Suicidal Self-Injury (NSSI): a narrative synthesis of associated variables and a meta-analysis of risk.' *Journal of Affective Disorders, 276*, 1159–1172. https://doi.org/10.1016/j.jad.2020.07.103.

Hooley, J.M. & Franklin, J.C. (2018). 'Why do people hurt themselves? A new conceptual model of nonsuicidal self-injury.' *Clinical Psychological Science, 6*(3), 428–451. https://doi.org/10.1177/2167702617745641.

Suicide

Casey, P., Dunn, G., Kelly, B.D., Lehtinen, V. *et al.* (2008). 'The prevalence of suicidal ideation in the general population: results from the Outcome of Depression International Network (ODIN) study.' *Social Psychiatry and Psychiatric Epidemiology, 43*, 299–304. https://doi.org/10.1007/s00127-008-0313-5.

King, M., Semlyen, J., Tai, S.S., Killaspy, H. *et al.* (2008). 'A systematic review of mental disorder, suicide, and deliberate self harm in lesbian, gay and bisexual people.' *BMC Psychiatry, 8*, 70. https://doi.org/10.1186/1471-244X-8-70.

Thoma, B.C., Salk, R.H., Choukas-Bradley, S., Goldstein, T.R., Levine, M.D. & Marshal, M.P. (2019). 'Suicidality disparities between transgender and cisgender adolescents.' *Pediatrics, 144*(5), e20191183. https://doi.org/10.1542/peds.2019-1183.